To my dear friends,
John and Maureen Roscoe
with love and best wishes
from the author.

Dick Chrisman

Fleurvoy, CA
5 June '03

An old time Western hunter's Remington Hepburn rifle with an array of Remington implements. It is chambered for the .45-2 7/8" Sharps cartridge—and weighs 13 1/4 pounds.

CARTRIDGE

RELOADING

TOOLS

OF THE

PAST

R. H. CHAMBERLAIN
TOM QUIGLEY

ISBN 0-9661334-0-4

Copies of this book are available from:

Tom Quigley
PO Box 1567
Castle Rock, WA 98611

E-mail: tlqmlq@kalama.com
Fax: 1-360-274-0920

Price:
$25 each
+ $ 2 per book for shipping and handling

Inquire about quantity prices

Printed by Walker Lithograph
Red Bluff, California

DEDICATION

The authors would like to dedicate this book to their wives, Judy Chamberlain and Marsha Quigley, who both encouraged and supported them in this endeavor. The authors would also like to express their appreciation to Marsha Quigley for her word processing skills which turned their "notes" into a book.

The authors are indebted to and grateful for the assistance provided by the following:

Harold Ball	William Loos
Lamar Bayles	George Lower
Raymond Bell Jr.	George McCluney
Richard Bennett	William McNally
Bob Borcherdt	Cleve Mulder
Bob Borie	Dennison Payne
Dennis Brooks	Al Perry
William Brophy	Michael Petrov
Ed Curtis	Jairo Plazas
Bill Deming	Gary Quinlan
Ken Descovich	Robin Rapley
Harry Dozier	Bill Richardson
John Dutcher	Gary Roedl
Jeff Edwards	Tom Rowe
Gene Farmer	Frank Sellers
Bill Frietas	Fred Selman
Henry Gier	Larry Shelton
Art Gogan	James Sones
Leo Goodwin	Gale Stockton
John Gross	Phil Wahl
Glenn Hockett	Eric Walker
Robert Holter	Phil White
George Hoyem	Terry White
G. Scott Jamieson	Tom Wibberly
Tom Johnson	Stanley Williamson
Joe Kimmel	Drury Williford Jr.
John Kleine	Lewis Yearout
Kenneth Knox	Lloyd Yost
John Kopec	Don Zuckswert
George Krienke	Jim Zupan

and any others who have contributed to this effort but who have been unintentionally omitted.

CONTENTS

INTRODUCTION

It was almost thirty years ago that *Early Loading Tools and Bullet Molds* was published drawing largely on the author's own modest though varied collection. It came about at the urging of the late George Lower. The writer had been collecting early tools and molds—they being far more affordable than antique firearms and a relatively unexplored niche in arms collecting. Following exploratory articles in *The Gun Report* and *Gun Digest* the first printing in 1970 of *Early Loading Tools and Bullet Molds* with photographs by Jeff Edwards and printing by Farm Tribune Press was self-published and dedicated to the memory of Henry Gier who "...early recognized and appreciated loading accessories as a worthwhile collecting interest." A second printing, containing an addendum, followed in 1977. The latest reprint in 1988 suffered in the quality of reproduction, some detail being lost. Additionally, there was a lot of new information to share. Thus it was time to approach the subject anew.

In the introduction to the earlier book the origin of the writer's collection was described—how a ten-cent "leather punch" from a roadside second-hand store cleaned up to reveal its identity as an Ideal tong loading tool for the tiny .22 Maynard extra long cartridge.

Since that book was launched in 1970, much has changed in the field of arms collecting. Immediately apparent is the increase in prices, particularly for finer specimens. Even more noteworthy is the proliferation of books and articles of increasing specialization. Gun shows have grown as well—some tawdry and of little interest to serious collectors, but others placing an increased emphasis on "display only" exhibits which are often of striking sophistication. Many of them feature artifacts such as cartridges and sometimes reloading implements related to the arms exhibited.

Another notable development for purposes of this volume is the increasing number of people who collect reloading tools and molds specifically. It was predicted in 1970 that their numbers were certain to grow and indeed that has occurred. One of those collectors focusing specifically on early reloading implements is Tom Quigley of Castle Rock, Washington, who has graciously agreed to be co-author of this study.

This volume is designed to be of value not only to those specialist collectors but also to arms collectors who want to know the reloading equipment appropriate to their respective fields. It can be valuable to any collector or dealer who occasionally encounters a loading item and wants to properly identify it, perhaps learning its relative scarcity and desirability for they are not necessarily the same. Cartridge collectors may find it useful as well.

It is always a pleasure to find that old tools and molds are not just savored but are also used in reloading obsolete cartridges. Except for pristine specimens, tools and molds can be used without substantial risk to their collectibility.

No claim is made that the selection of tools and molds shown and described here is exhaustive. One collection of Ideal tools alone numbers in the hundreds. Many, of course, differ only in caliber while others reflect not only the variety of models but design changes in them. In order to be useful to a broad range of readers yet still be an affordable, usable handbook, minor variations have not been illustrated and some not mentioned. It must be borne in mind that the manufacturers, especially in the last century, would make almost anything the customer wanted. Also, gunsmiths and shooters produced implements of their own designs, thus helping to account for the innumerable variations encountered, some almost unique. You will not find all of them here. The choice to include or not is ours alone, and the authors make no apology for inclusion or omission.

The problem of delimitation, relatively easy when dealing with the product of a single company, had to be addressed. We have chosen to begin with the fully self-contained reloadable cartridges that appeared shortly after the Civil War. Where to stop was more difficult. Certainly the bulk of the implements here are from the black powder era though many carried over into the smokeless powder period. Our stopping point is somewhere in the early twentieth century. The fascinating field of shotshell and foreign reloading tools has been left for other researchers to explore.

Finally, it should be noted that some items unidentified in *Early Loading Tools and Bullet Molds* have since been identified while others have a tentative identification.

We trust the reader will find this effort useful. Its crafting has been a pleasurable undertaking, thanks in large part to the gracious help and cooperation of the dedicated arms collecting fraternity.

R. H. Chamberlain
Flournoy, California
1997

I

A BRIEF HISTORY OF HANDLOADING

In any overview of hand reloading it must be immediately noted that all muzzle-loading arms are hand loaded, normally with loose powder and ball or shot. During the muzzle-loading era, military arms increasingly utilized prepared paper cartridges containing the bullet or sometimes "buck and ball" and a premeasured powder charge to be rammed down the barrel; but the method of ignition, whether by flintlock or percussion cap, including Maynard's tape primers, continued to be entirely separate and external to the charge. Most noteworthy is the famous Minié ball cartridge so extensively used in our own American Civil War.

Wars, however terrible their effects, do stimulate inventiveness. This was especially true in the four years of the American Civil war and the period immediately leading up to it. At its beginning, the regular Army was quite small and ill prepared to do battle on any significant scale as demonstrated at the first battle of Bull Run (Manassas). To cope with the arms shortage the federal government scoured its own arsenals and those of Europe. In an effort to be sure that "their boys" were suitably equipped, northern states looked to the commercial arms market both in the United States and abroad. The South acted similarly. Anyone with guns to sell or an idea of how to make them could get a contract. Often enthusiasm and patriotism triumphed over good sense, and many never reached fruition. Others only got into serious production by war's end; thus accounting for many collector arms found in practically new condition today.

Most of the Civil War breech loaders, at least initially, fired externally-primed cartridges. But fully self-contained rimfire cartridges gradually entered the picture in arms like the Sharps and Hankins and the Henry but most notably the Spencer repeater. Also small rimfire handguns such as the Smith and Wesson were available for private purchase as personal weapons. By the end of hostilities it was apparent, even to the conservative hierarchy in the ordnance department, that the era of the muzzle loading military rifle was over. With huge inventories of these suddenly obsolete arms there was a rush to convert them to breech loaders, and the era of the familiar "trapdoor" Springfield began. The civilian market was stimulated as well to turn to cartridge arms. As the limitations of rimfire cartridges became apparent, centerfire cartridges came to the fore. There is no better illustration than that in the single year of 1873 the famous Winchester .44-40, the Colt Single Action .45 revolver, and the government .45-70 appeared—all centerfires.

In the late 1860's reloading centerfire cartridges began to appear using the primer developed by Col. Hiram Berdan of Civil War Sharpshooters fame. It was essentially a broad, shallow percussion cap of somewhat heavier gauge metal. The anvil, against which the fulminate of mercury must be crushed by the firing pin blow to supply the fire igniting the powder, is part of the case head itself. The flash enters the case through small holes surrounding the anvil. It was a viable system until the time came to remove the primer for reloading. With no center flash hole, the primer, still called a 'cap' as in percussion lock muzzle loader days, had to be picked out of its pocket. This entailed piercing it with a chisel-like devise, the simplest being a cap awl, and prying it out. Those who have decapped this way can testify to its frustrations. Many old-time reloading tools are equipped to remove Berdan primers. It should be mentioned that there were a few cases designed for Berdan primers having a central flash hole. James Grant shows one in a Ballard caliber in his classic *Single Shot Rifles*.

When the Winchester Model 1873 rifle appeared, one of its distinctive features was that it employed a new cartridge, the .44 Winchester Centerfire, often shortened to .44 WCF but soon better known by its alliterative appellation .44-40, the second figure designating the powder charge. It replaced the .44 Henry rimfire cartridge used in the Model 1866 Winchester. Not only was it a bit more powerful, it utilized a cleaner bullet that carried its lubricant inside the case; and its boxer-type primer made reloading them feasible. The primer could be forced out by means of a decapping pin pushed through the central flash hole in the way that has become the standard in American cartridges whether destined for reloading or not. Some primer tins and boxes are shown in (A) and (B).

A

B

Many early cartridges were loaded with "heel" bullets in which the base or "heel" of the bullet had a reduced diameter which fit the inside of the case while the forward part of the bullet was of the same diameter as the outside of the case. After loading in a dry state, the protruding part of the bullet was dipped in melted lubricant. The major drawback to the greasy lubricants used at that time was that they picked up lint and dirt. This design is still seen in the common .22 rimfire of today. Most modern loadings have resolved this problem by using a hard lubricating material.

The black gunpowder of the time used a formula centuries old and most products were ballistically quite similar, the difference being mostly in the granulation size and thoroughness of the mixing of the ingredients in the milling process. For handloading purposes it was put up in canisters. Mostly these were of one-pound and half-pound size. A few were in the shape of the familiar muzzle-loader powder flask. Often the labels were colorful and these canisters have become collectible in their own right. A selection of them is shown in (C).

C

Since black powders were so similar in the pressure produced by a given volume, they were ordinarily measured by dipping. Most dippers were of a fixed capacity and they were often stamped with the charge weight. A representative group of them is shown in (D). All are for a single charge and not adjustable except one by Laflin and Rand which has a screw in the side to allow for adjustment. It is graduated in increments of 1/16 dram but is for smokeless powder. The dram measurement was a carryover from black powder, and a few early smokeless powder canisters carried loading data using this quaint measurement.

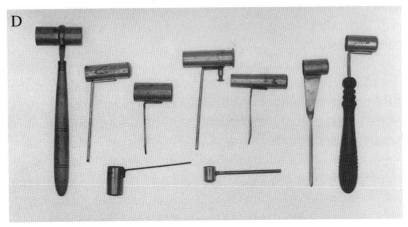

D

Most muzzle-loading sporting rifles used a greased cloth patch which wrapped around the ball as it was rammed down the barrel. Compressed into the rifling, it made the ball spin without deforming it, lubricated its passage, served as a seal to prevent powder gasses from wasting their force, and even cleaned and softened the powder fouling. Some muzzle-loading rifles made for target purposes used a cylindrical bullet with a patch made of two or three strips of oiled paper criss-crossing the muzzle. Like the cloth patch, they enveloped the bullet as it passed down the bore. The idea of a paper patch carried over to metallic cartridges in the form best known in the large caliber Sharps and Remington loads made famous on the 1000 yard Creedmoor range and by buffalo hunters on the plains. With these the paper patch was cut in the shape of a parallelogram to twice encircle a smooth lead bullet. A small amount of tin was added to the bullet alloy for hardness and to assure better casting. The tail end of the patch could be twisted up and tucked into the hollow base of the bullet. The bullets were loaded and fired dry, but a thin wad of lubricant was often used behind it with a card wad to separate it from the powder charge. Although bullet molds were available to cast these bullets and swages could be used to assure their uniformity, the process was tedious; and many shooters simply purchased them ready-made by factories which employed large numbers of young women to patch them. An assortment of factory-made bullet boxes is shown in (E). Also cases could be purchased empty. See (F). Cartridges were sometimes designated especially for reloading. Some boxes even contained loading data. See (G).

E

    There were a number of attractions to handloading ammunition. One was cost. The most expensive component of a cartridge was the brass case which required many operations to manufacture but was essentially undamaged in firing. Another factor had to do with the availability of ammunition. Many arms companies had at least some cartridges of their own design. There were, for example, at least three separate versions of the .32-40 cartridge, the familiar one for Ballard, Marlin, and Winchester plus different ones by both Bullard and Remington. None would interchange. Another example is the .40-70 with differing treatments by Ballard, Winchester, Maynard, Peabody, and Sharps; the last seen in both bottleneck- and straight-case types. Furthermore, the companies sometimes chambered for a competitor's cartridge. It was often difficult to find a supply of uncommon ammunition under ordinary circumstances and even more difficult on the frontier. The surest way to have proper ammunition was to get a good supply of empty cases or factory loads and load or reload them. Primers, lead, and powder were obtainable everywhere to "roll your own" ammunition. Finally, there was the fact that the shooter could fine-tune his load to his own firearm or even reduce it markedly for short-range and/or the popular indoor "gallery" shooting.

F

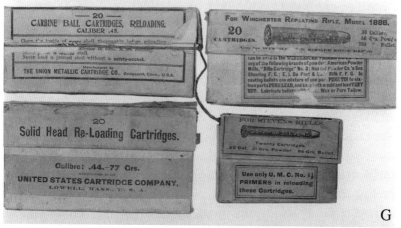

G

Even with the relatively low pressures of black powder loads, cases did wear out usually by enlargement of the primer pocket in the days before the "solid head" case came along. Paper patched bullets were not crimped, but most others were and that shortened case life. One solution to the former was the "everlasting" case. While having the same outside dimensions as regular cases, they were half again as heavy with most of the extra metal being in the head. The mouth had to be thin enough to accept the regular diameter bullet. They were available in a variety of calibers from .32-35 Maynard to .45-70 Government. Then there were special ones with very thick mouths requiring their own separate chambering. One such is the .40-90 Ballard Ideal Everlasting which was not at all interchangeable with any other cartridge including the regular .40-90 Ballard. Everlasting cases were expensive and were sold singly at several cents apiece, a goodly amount at the time. Some were nickel plated to reduce corrosion, improve extraction, and, no doubt, to impress the shooter. They do make a handsome load.

The formula for gunpowder, called black powder since the advent of smokeless powder, has remained unchanged over the centuries. Improved quality was usually a function of the milling process, cheaper grades requiring less treatment. But near the end of the 19th century smokeless powders began to come to the market for both factory loading and hand loaders. Immediately there was a serious problem. The new powders were very dense, a given volume producing much more pressure than a similar charge of black powder. Some shooters did not read and follow the loading data and proceeded to measure it out in their regular black powder dippers. Many burst barrels and revolver cylinders resulted. Handloading, especially with smokeless powder, came into disfavor. This was quickly rectified by the production of "bulk" smokeless powders. They were almost fluffy in texture and could be loaded with regular black powder measures. Another development was semi-smokeless powder which could be similarly loaded. Soon shooters learned that a small amount of smokeless powder on top of the primer followed by black powder for the balance of the charge gave clean shooting and often improved accuracy over straight black powder. They came to be known as "duplex" loads and were a favorite among target rifle shooters around the turn of the century. Special mechanical powder measures were devised for this kind of loading and one early Ideal shotshell charger was even promoted as also suitable for loading <u>three</u> different powders in the same charge using the shot hopper to supplement the black and smokeless ones! This company brought out the well-known and highly useful *Ideal Handbook* which has gone through dozens of editions since its appearance in the 19th century serving as a combination catalog and instruction manual.

This overview is only an introduction to the story of handloading cartridges to set the stage for a better understanding of the information which follows as we explore the various makes and models of cartridge reloading tools. For additional information, the reader is referred to Phil Sharpe's classic *Complete Guide to Handloading*.

II

WINCHESTER

Even a cursory examination of old-time reloading tools and bullet molds at gun shows, on dealer's lists, and in collections shows us that two manufacturers account for the vast majority of them. These are the Winchester Repeating Arms Company and the Ideal Manufacturing Company. In this chapter we take up the former with the Ideal line to be examined in a later one.

There are several reasons for the large number of Winchester tools and molds. First, their rifles dominated the American arms industry in the later part of the 19th century and on into the 20th. The majority of their 19th century arms were centerfire and thus their ammunition could be reloaded.

Second, Winchester began to offer reloading tools almost from the inception of their centerfire rifles and featured them extensively in their catalogs and advertising.

Third, they produced these tools and molds in a great variety of calibers, for those of other manufacturers as well as their own.

Fourth, their products were sturdy and effective. They worked.

Finally, they continuously developed their line of reloading implements over the years with new designs and modifications of existing ones.

Students of the Winchester line of reloading tools and molds owe a debt to Lewis E. Yearout for researching them and sharing the information with fellow collectors in the monograph, *Winchester Reloading Tools*, published by the Winchester Arms Collectors Association in 1982. His work has been helpful in the preparation of this chapter.

Winchester's first rifle, the Model 1866, fired a .44 caliber rimfire cartridge carried over from the Henry rifle and thus was not reloadable.

The introduction of the Model 1873 rifle, firing a centerfire cartridge, made reloading its ammunition feasible. Its cartridge was the famous .44 Winchester Centerfire, abbreviated to .44 WCF and also known as the .44-40-200 to indicate both its powder charge and bullet weight as was customary at the time. After well over a century, it is still with us. So is its primer, the one familiar to all handloaders, which carries its own anvil against which the priming compound is crushed by the blow of the firing pin. This concussion caused its detonation and the resulting flash passed through a hole in the center of the primer pocket into the powder charge igniting it and propelling the bullet through the barrel. What made this cartridge case easily reloadable was its central flash hole which permitted the use of a decapping pin to force the primer out from the inside. Within a year Winchester produced its first reloading tool.

The first Winchester reloading tool was the subject of an article in the January 1992 issue of *The Gun Report*. Briefly stated it was based upon a patent granted to W. W. Winchester, son of the company founder, on October 20, 1874. The tool was of the "nutcracker" variety which was to become the standard for most Winchester tools and those of other manufacturers. This first tool was distinguished by its two "studs" or "standards" jutting up from the lower portion of the tool. One of them has a protruding pin to expel the fired primer while the other has a dished top to accommodate the primer pocket while the new primer is seated. An example of this first Winchester tool is shown in (A).

A

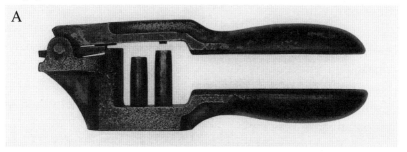

Like other early Winchester tools and those of some other companies, it was of cast iron which, though inexpensive, is brittle resulting in the broken handles found on some of these tools. Cast iron, having a rough surface, makes a good base for a painted finish. Apparently, the earliest tools had a black "Japanned" finish with no markings whatsoever. This was followed by the addition of the patent date cast into the tool's upper handle. The last of them had a gold painted finish (after all this was the "guilded age") and carried the patent date in the same location. Though the contours changed over time, this patent was to be utilized by Winchester for its basic reloading tool right up to their discontinuance about 1914. There is no caliber marking on these first tools as the model 1873 Rifle was made in only one caliber. Even the company name was absent though some of these tools reportedly carry a very tiny assembly number. They were sold either separately or in a boxed set that included a bullet mold, charge cup, and wad cutter. Wads were useful between bullet and powder to keep the lubricant from damaging the powder charge. This pioneering tool was on the market for approximately a year, and while advertised as available for a variety of cartridges, only specimens in .44 WCF are known to the writers.

Next in the Winchester line of loading tools was the one with its box shown in (B). The "studs" had been abandoned and the shape much streamlined; but it still was made of cast iron,

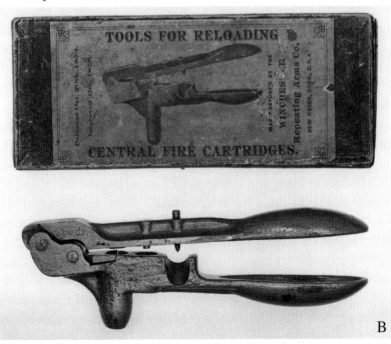

B

had spoon-shaped handles, and was painted gold. It was based on the same patent as the first tool. This patent date appears on the box together with "Improved OCT. 1875." A separate decapping pin was furnished with each tool. A few early ones bear tiny numbers near the hinge junction. The company called it the "Improved Loader": and like the first tool, it has the patent date cast in; but, in addition, had the caliber stamped on the upper handle. This became necessary because some of these tools were produced in calibers other than .44 WCF. The accompanying instruction sheet is shown in (C). Some, reportedly the earlier versions, had a chisel and frame cutout for extracting Berdan primers. They were first marketed in October 1875 and were last listed in the spring of 1879. Those without the Berdan chisel continued until 1882.

At this point it should be noted that there have been several charts prepared that catalogue Winchester's line of tools; probably the best and most recent by Lewis E. Yearout. These sources can be very useful but can also lead to confusion among collectors as a result of their differences in nomenclature. Besides, items at the factory and the warehouse did not necessarily square with the catalogs and were never as orderly as later collectors would prefer. Accordingly, we will stick primarily to patent dates, illustrations, and descriptions in our discussion of Winchester tools.

A big brother to the "Improved Loader" is shown in (D). It is a massive affair weighing just short of three pounds and was designed to load larger cartridges. It was made necessary by the introduction of the Winchester Model 1876 or "Centennial" rifle initially available only in .45-75 WCF. This tool is in that caliber and bears the stamping "45 75 WCF" on a flat near the hinge. It was available in other calibers as well. Note that it carries the Berdan decapping chisel which can be screwed in and out to properly engage the primer in the cartridge held in the angled cutout. The very comfortable spoon-shaped handles were carried on from earlier models, as was the gold painted finish.

The patent dated September 14, 1880 was the basis for a series of tools that differed significantly from their predecessors

C

INSTRUCTIONS FOR USING

WINCHESTER'S

Cartridge Reloading Tools.

———•———

To remove the Primer, place the primer extracting plug inside of the shell, so that the pin will enter the hole in the head of the shell ; then place the shell with plug into the die, and by pressing the handles together, force out the primer.

To insert new Primer, start it squarely into the pocket by hand, then put the shell into the hole through the lower lever, and press the primer home by bringing the levers together.

To load the Cartridge, put in the shell the charge cup full of powder, and on the top of this place such wads or lubricants as the kind of cartridge may require ; start in the ball by hand, then having placed it in the die, bring the handles together by a steady pressure, and the cartridge will be finished and swaged to the original size. Remove the cartridge from the die by opening the levers with a sharp, quick motion.

To prevent the cartridge from sticking in the die, a drop of oil should be put in it occasionally.

——— • ———

CAUTION.

In order that a good reloaded cartridge may be made, the shells designed to be used should be thoroughly washed as soon as possible after they have been fired, as the burnt powder will corrode the brass shell and ruin it.

D

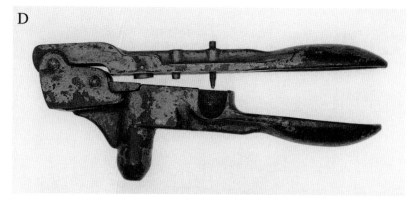

in two immediately apparent ways. One is the switch from gold painted cast iron to forged, polished and blued steel. Unlike the earlier cast iron tools, these were not brittle. The other major difference was the method of extracting the completed cartridge from the seating/crimping chamber. Following the patent specifications, a pair of claws, part of the upper handle, engaged the cartridge rim to lift it out.

A less obvious but patented feature of this model is a pivoting "pressing block" on the upper handle which forced the assembled cartridge into the seating chamber. This feature allowed the tool's leverage to be almost doubled without risking a bent case. This and other features of Winchester and other makes of tools may be better understood by referring to the various patent drawings in the Appendix.

It was the patent for this tool, incidentally, which led to the association of John Browning with Winchester. The Browning brothers of Ogden, Utah Territory had been producing a reloading tool for the local trade which inadvertently infringed upon the V. A. King patent held by Winchester. An agreement was worked out to the satisfaction of both parties. In addition, their long and productive relationship had begun.

The earliest versions of this 1880 tool featured the familiar spoon-shaped handles of the earlier tools. A specimen of this tool in .50-70 Government caliber with its original box, mold, decapping pin, and powder dipper is shown in (E). The earlier tools still bore no company name but the later ones did. At least one of these tools has been reported with "N.W.M.P." markings

E

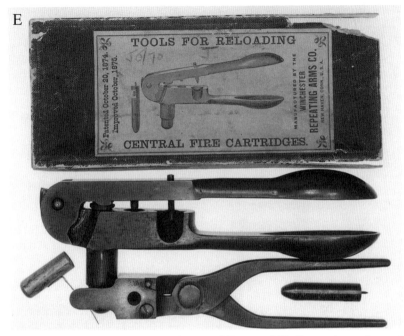

indicating use by the Northwest Mounted Police who adopted the Winchester Model 1876 carbine in .45-75 WCF.

In his book, *Tools, Targets, and Troopers,* James Zupan tells of the U.S. Army's trial of the 1880 tool especially constructed with holes drilled into the seating/crimping chamber to release excess bullet lubricant. But, the military concluded that the government-issued arsenal tools were superior. One problem was that the Winchester tool did not full length resize the case and some reloads were oversize for the rifle's chamber. Furthermore, given the scale of military reloading, the arsenal tools were faster. One of these marked "Co B" and "U.S." and having the extra holes in the die is shown in (F) and (G).

F

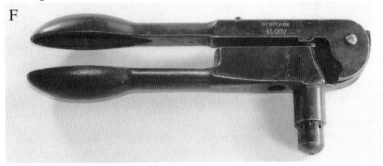

G

Probably as a way of reducing the cost of manufacturing, the spoon handles were soon replaced by plain ones of the same width as the rest of the tool. This model is, like earlier ones, found with and without the Berdan chisel feature as shown in (H). A very few, like this specimen are found with adjustable chambers rather than the standard integral ones. These chambers or dies were held in adjustment by a knurled lock ring much like those on the familiar Ideal tong tools.

One reason for the discontinuance of this model may have been that in order to get the extractor claws close enough to the

H

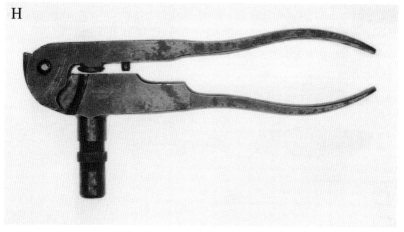

chamber, the walls of the latter had to be beveled almost to a knife edge making it subject to damage. Still, its great leverage and ability to handle large cartridges kept it around into the 1890s when replaced by a whole new class of Winchester tools.

The tool generally called the Model 1882 was based on the November 7 patent of that year plus the earlier 1874 patent. Actually the 1882 patent referred to the improved decapping pin which had a flare on it to expand the case mouth slightly, removing the old crimp to prevent the bullet from wrinkling the case. The patentee was none other than John Barlow who went on to found the famous Ideal line of reloading tools. He also incorporated this idea into his tools. Other than this feature, the 1882 tool was designed around the 1874 patent but in polished and blued steel. One of these tools and its box are shown in (I). This model continued in the Winchester line until the company discontinued the sale of all loading tools, circa 1914. Some speculate that accidents caused by the improper loading of smokeless powder charges brought about this decision.

Before we leave the 1882 tool, it should be mentioned that a few, like some 1880 tools, were made with an adjustable

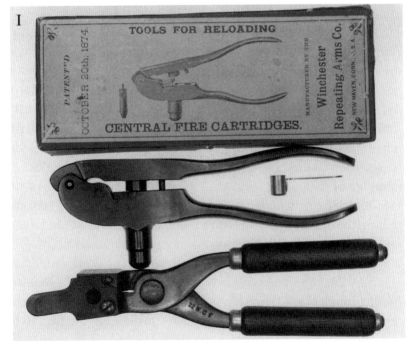

I

seating chamber. They may be found with either round or oblong inspection windows or none at all. These openings allowed the reloader to see how the bullet was starting into the neck of the case. This was particularly desirable when loading paper patched bullets to assure that the patches were not torn or wrinkled in the seating process. See (J).

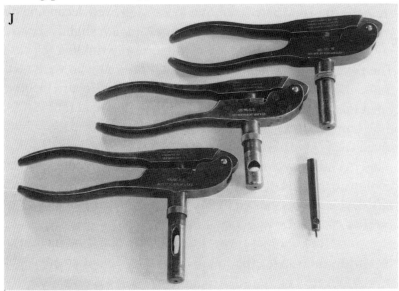

The final three loading tools introduced by Winchester were designed to full length resize the case while the bullet was being seated and crimped in place. There were two very good reasons for doing so. First, cartridge cases, particularly large ones, could expand or stretch with continued use becoming difficult to extract from the rifle's chamber after firing. Second, the chambers of firearms of the same caliber vary slightly so that cases fired in one rifle would not necessarily fit the chamber of another of that same caliber. Probably the introduction of the Model 1886 rifle with its array of powerful cartridges played some part in the decision to bring out a tool that would resize the loaded cartridge down to the dimensions of new, unfired ones.

The first and scarcest of these new tools was patented on January 24, 1888 and is shown in (K). It is an ungainly monster with a rough black finish having two pivoting arms and a removable die which is unfortunately easily lost. This die had to be

K

removed from the body of the tool to allow the case to be put in place for recapping. One arm pivoted to seat the primer. The assembled cartridge went into the die chamber and the other handle turned until it stopped at which point the completed cartridge was ready to be removed by reversing the process. Obviously it was a slow and awkward procedure, but it did do the job and, with hunting cartridges, production speed was of little consequence. The tool's caliber was stamped on its die which is interchangeable so other cartridges calibers, with the same size case head, could be reloaded in that tool.

A supposed improvement on the 1888 tool was patented March 17, 1891 and is shown with its box in (L). It is of polished, blued steel. Though relatively scarce, they are more frequently encountered than the Model 1888. Its instruction sheet is shown in (M) but nothing substitutes for actual use of this remarkable tool. The cases were first decapped using a strange and intricate "L" shaped pin. Then the case was placed in a slot on the tool and the other end of the decapper rotated to seat the primer. The handles were partly unscrewed and the assembled cartridge placed through one handle and into the die in the other. A left-handed threaded, knurled piece was screwed in place and the handles rotated forcing the cartridge into the die which was part of the opposite handle. Then the handles were unscrewed releasing the completed cartridge. Note that the cartridge was not put directly into the die or it would stick in place presenting a dangerous job of removal. Along with the caliber marking, in

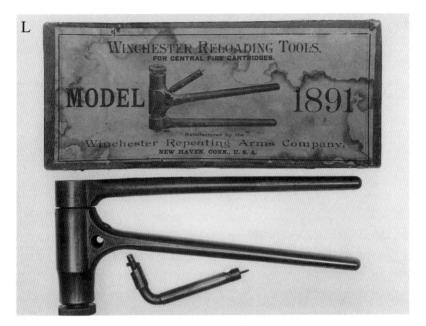

WINCHESTER RELOADING TOOLS,
FOR CENTRAL FIRE CARTRIDGES.

MODEL 1891

Manufactured by the
Winchester Repeating Arms Company,
NEW HAVEN, CONN., U. S. A.

large letters, is the warning "KEEP THE DIE CLEAN."

Like the Model 1888 tool, the 1891 had a short life. Its ingenious but complicated design required skilled machining and careful polishing but in operation it was still slow and awkward. It was soon replaced by another full length resizing tool, but this time Winchester got it right and this tool was to remain in their catalogs until production of all tools ceased about 1914. Both it and the Model 1882 survived to the end.

This tool, the Model 1894, was far superior to those of 1888 and 1891. It was simple, less awkward to operate, compact, and the dies easily interchanged. From a manufacturing standpoint, they must have been much less expensive. A specimen of this tool with its box is shown in (N). It was supplied with decapping pin, charge cup (powder dipper), and bullet mold or in a smaller box without the mold for those who might be using factory-made bullets. The decapping pin was dropped into the empty case and knocked out with a gentle rap from a mallet. Recapping was performed by placing the case in a receptacle at the upper end of the tool and closing the handle. The arms companies would go to great lengths to satisfy customers. One of these tools has been reported in .42 Russian Berdan caliber which

MODEL 1891 RELOADING TOOL.

MANUFACTURED BY THE

WINCHESTER REPEATING ARMS CO.,

New Haven, Conn., U. S. A.

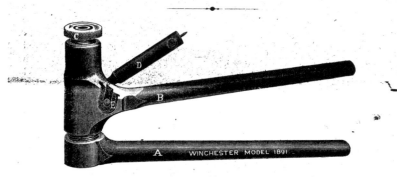

This tool extracts the spent primer, inserts the new one, reloads and resizes the cartridge. It consists of four pieces, and its use may be readily understood by examining the cut.

Part "D" (the extractor plug), is furnished with a point to knock out the primer, and serves to insert the new primer, as hereinafter described.

Part "C" is a nut with a *left-handed* screw, which is removed to place the cartridge in the die, and which is replaced to hold the same during the process of loading. It is furnished with a groove, serving to straighten the mouth of the shell.

Part "B" when turned about the die "A," by means of its handle, carries the nut "C" down upon "A," forcing the contained cartridge into the die "A."

Part "A" carries the sizing and reloading die, and is furnished with a handle as shown. This die is the vital part of the tool. The greatest care is taken to make it to the exact size and to give it a fine finish. It should be kept clean and free from rust.

To extract the Primer. Detach the extractor plug "D" from part "B." Put the shell upon the handle "D." Its point will extend into the vent of the shell. Rap the head of the shell diagonally upon a block of wood, table or other solid object which will not dent the shell, and the primer will fall out.

To insert the Primer. Place the head of the shell in the slot "E." Place the primer in the groove which is in the part "B," back of the head of the shell, and it will drop in place in front of the pocket. Turn the handle "D" to the right until the primer is in place. Do not use force to do this, but seat the primer gently, and see that its surface is below the surface of the head of the shell. Do the priming with clean hands, and see that the pocket in the shell is clean.

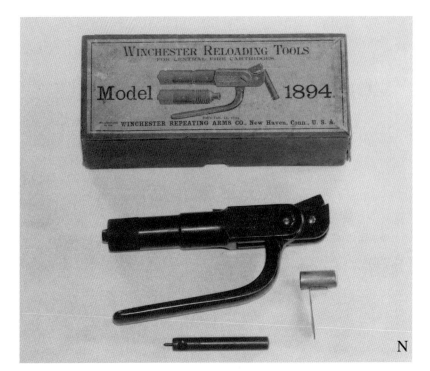

has a chisel primer extractor for removing the Berdan caps. It is apparently factory made. Another is marked "44-77P" indicating that it is designed for loading that early Sharps and Remington round using paper patched bullets which are not crimped. A special reamer may have been required for just this one order. This was an era of company pride and customer loyalty.

To seat and crimp the bullet and full length size the case in the Model 1894 tool, the primed and charged case with bullet started into the case neck was placed in the die and the latter hand-turned until it stopped. Then alternately closing the handle and turning the die, the cartridge was forced all the way into the die. Since there was great leverage exerted due to the design of the mechanism, the process was an easy one and relatively speedy as well.

The Model 1894 tool was designed to load cartridges from .236 U.S. Navy to .50-100-450 Winchester Express, while pistol and small rifle cartridges continued to be loaded in the Model 1882 tool. It should be noted that Winchester tools have no provision for bullet sizing. Their molds cast bullets of the correct diameter to fire as cast.

While we have documentation on the earliest Winchester loading tools, the situation with bullet molds of the same period is not nearly as clear. The company really preferred that reloaders use factory made bullets, not just because it brought in additional revenue but also because the customer was more likely to be satisfied with the results. When they did begin to furnish molds, they were of a type almost guaranteed to produce customer dissatisfaction though surely not intended to do so. The earliest Winchester molds cast bullets without a lubricating groove which required them to be hand dipped in lubricant. Bullet lubricants of the time were not the neat dry types found on modern .22 rimfires today but were formulated of tallow, beeswax, and other natural substances which picked up lint, grit, and the like. These earliest molds are virtually identical to the Sharps Rifle Company brass, one-piece molds as illustrated in plates (C) and (D) of the Sharps chapter. This striking similarity prompted Yearout to speculate that they may have been a Sharps product. The bullet simply dropped out of the upturned mold. No lubricating grooves were possible with such a design. These rare molds bear no markings. Shortly after their introduction, an improved version came out that was quite similar except that it incorporated a turned wooden handle fitted to a tang to make them more pleasant to use. Brass is a great conductor of heat, and bullet casting with the first type must have been unpleasant if not down right painful. The second type does carry the caliber stamped on the side of the mold. The introduction of Winchester's Model 1876 rifle with its .45-75 cartridge made this stamping necessary. One of these rare molds is shown in (O).

Next for consideration is a mold previously unidentified. Now it has at least tentative identification as an early Winchester

O

product. Pointing to it are several clues. First is that the few encountered are generally in the earliest Winchester calibers of .44 WCF and .45-75 WCF. Second, they are of the same material, brass, used in the other early Winchester molds. Third, the handles are similar to the single one on the mold just described. One of these suspected Winchester molds, bearing no marking other than "45-75" stamped into its side, is shown in (P). Being a two-piece mold allowed the casting of grooved bullets. Finally, pointing to its Winchester identity, its successor, to be described next, is also of brass, of two-piece design, and has only its caliber marked. Thus it follows in a natural progression. Considering all these factors it seems reasonable to at least tentatively identify it as a Winchester product until a better case can be made for something else.

P

The next mold, like the others so far described, is not pictured in any Winchester catalog or other known company literature. This is not surprising as molds were seen primarily as an ordinary adjunct to the more complex (and patentable) tools. This brass or bronze mold has the distinct shape that would characterize all the Winchester molds that followed. While not so rare as the previous models, they are not common. Their only markings are the caliber and, on some, tiny assembly numbers. Calibers are stamped on the flat upper surface of one handle. They were made in a variety of calibers in addition to the Winchester line. The specimen shown here in (Q) is clearly marked "44 77 395." The last number denotes the bullet weight in grains in the manner of the times. This one casts grooved bullets but, along with some other calibers, could be ordered for a paper patched bullet.

Q

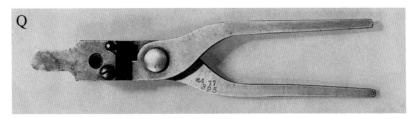

The mold shown in (R), clearly evolved from the one just described, is fully marked with the company's name and location as well as the caliber. The entire mold is of highly polished and blued steel. To again illustrate the great variety available, the one shown here is marked "32-185 SLUG." It makes a smooth paper patched bullet for the standard .32-40 cartridge, the slightly heavier than customary weight being desirable for target shooting. Reportedly, these were designed for swaging in a die before patching as was done with target bullets from other makers. These molds made no provision for protecting the caster's hands but the tapered handles did lend themselves to home-made handles which allowed for some protection. As with all previous Winchester molds, these were not pictured in company catalogs. The earliest of these all-steel molds differed in having no alignment pin and no company name. The caliber was individually hand stamped in the usual location using small dies. Production of this all-steel style ceased about 1889.

R

Finally, we come to the last and most commonly encountered of the Winchester molds and the only one to be illustrated by the manufacturer. It was first illustrated in the June, 1890 Winchester Catalog. One is shown in (S). Essentially this was the previous model but it had neatly-made wooden handles having brass ferrules and held in place by a special screw in the end of each handle. This mold, like the Model 1882 and 1894 tools,

was produced until Winchester ceased selling loading implements.

A hollow point attachment is shown in (T). Hollow point bullets were designed to expand easily upon striking game and were often called "express" type due to their often being lighter than the standard bullet. Winchester hollow point molds are not common and the attachments are rarely encountered.

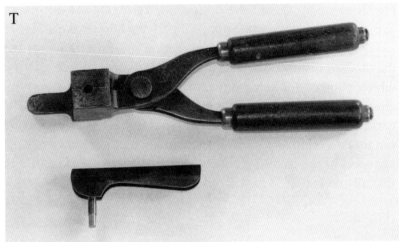

Still a further illustration of the company's willingness to cater to its customers is seen in (U). It is a two-cavity .22 WCF mold with each bullet slightly different in contour and two sprue cutters.

Also, Winchester sold blank molds for those wanting to "cherry" them to their own design. They even sold unmarked ones. Winchester molds have been observed stamped "S. D. & G." denoting sale by Schoverling, Daley, and Gales, a New York concern. Apparently Marlin bought some too as they are seen with that company's "M. F. A. Co." marking or just the caliber "40-M" but no reference to Winchester, the obvious maker. Those examined to date are of the earlier, iron-handled variety.

We conclude the Winchester chapter with an identification chart (V) prepared by the late Ray Bell.

V

WINCHESTER LOADING TOOL AND BULLET MOLD
IDENTIFICATION CHART

DESCRIPTION OF MODEL OR TYPE	NAME GIVEN BY COMPANY, PER CAT.	PATENT DATES	*CATALOG LISTINGS	
			FIRST	LAST
1. Cast Iron – per original patent design	"The Reloading Tool"	Oct. 20, 1874	1875–1st Edition	See note A
2. Cast Iron – modified, and with Berdan decapper	"Improved Reloader"	Oct. 20, 1874	1875–2nd Edition	May 1, 1879 (See note B)
3. Cast Iron – same as above, without Berdan decapper	Probably continued as "Imporved Reloader"	Oct. 20, 1874	May 1, 1879	April 1, 1882 (See note C)
4. Blued steel – lever type, with or without Berdan decapper	See note D	Sept. 14, 1880	Jan. 1, 1884 (See note C)	Cat. No. 56 Jan., 1896
5. Blued steel – lever type, without Berdan decapper	"The Lever Tool"	Oct. 20, 1874 Nov. 7, 1882	Sept. 1, 1882	Cat. No 79 1914
6. Cast steel – black Japanned finish; two levers – interchange- able dies	"The New Model"	Jan 24, 1888	Feb., 1889	July,, 1890
7. Blued steel – two levers, left- handed thread cap and right- angle capper-decapper	"Model 1891"	Mar. 17, 1891	March, 1891	Oct., 1893
8. Blued steel – single lever, screw-in die	"Model 1894"	Feb. 13, 1894	Cat. No. 52 April, 1894	Cat. No. 79 1914

WINCHESTER TOOL NOTATIONS

Note A: T. E. Hall, Curator Winchester Gun Museum,
says this tool last listed in 1875, 2nd edition, yet Parsons,
page 111, *The First Winchester,* shows it in what is supposed to be an 1878 catalog page reprint.

Note B: A separate Winchester, or pin type, decapper
came with most of the Berdan chisel equipped tools.

Note C: Per catalogs, this tool was superseded by "The
Lever Tool," though the model patented September 14,
1880, may have been made and sold to the trade prior to its
first listing in the January 1, 1884 issue. Such things did
happen, even in the case of guns.

Note D: For years this tool, together with "The Lever Tool," was
listed simply as "Tools For Reloading Central Fire Cartridges." When it was discontinued, the remaining one was
designated "The Lever Tool."

* Notice that some catalogs are designated by number
and date, others by date only. This is correct. A numbering
system seems to have been carried in the company books in some
way, yet the first issue actually numbered appears to be No. 52,
April, 1894.

[Compiled by Raymond Bell, Jr.]

III

REMINGTON, U. M. C., and B. G. I.

Because of the business connections of these three companies, their products will be considered together in this chapter. The connection of the first two is apparent when we see the familiar "REM-UMC" cartridge headstamps used until recent years. In addition, the "U" on Remington rimfire cartridges is a recognition of the involvement with U. M. C. Co. The Bridgeport Gun Implement Company connection comes about through its formation by the Union Metallic Cartridge Company to manufacture tools for cartridge reloading as well as other gun-related items such as cleaning rods, hunting knives, and compasses. They also dealt in the "traps" used to release live pigeons as shotgun targets, the original "trap shooting." The basic Remington story of how young Eliphalet Remington began by making rifle barrels is familiar to most collectors. Later he founded E. Remington and Sons which, in 1888, became the Remington Arms Company. The Union Metallic Cartridge Company was created in 1867 by Schuyler, Hartley, and Graham of New York.

We will begin with Remington tools and at the outset it should be noted that none of those examined by the authors bear the company name. Consequently their identification has been primarily through catalog illustrations, cased or boxed outfits, or by having accompanied Remington arms over the years.

Probably the first of the Remington tools for removing and replacing primers is the strange device shown in (A). It was until recently unidentified but now its identity seems certain. It

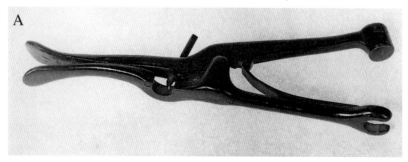

A

has the familiar black painted or "Japanned" finish. Made for decapping Berdan primed cases only, it has the usual chisel decapper with the depth adjustable by screwing it in or out of the tool handle. There is a built-in spring return. The broad, hammer-shaped end of one handle used for pressing the primer in place has a convex face to assure the primer being seated below the level of the head and solidly in its pocket. These tools are very scarce and were probably succeeded by the more conventionally shaped tool shown in (B). It too has a black finish. While the previous tool is without markings, this one bears the patent date of April 6th, 1875 and the nominal caliber, in this case "50." The place chosen to stamp it is in the channel which holds the

B

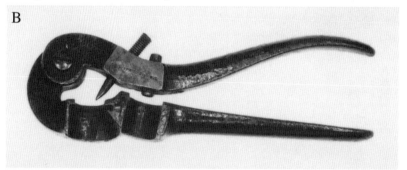

case for decapping. What with hand stamping on a curved surface and with the black paint often covering it, this marking is easy to miss. This tool is quite scarce and was probably succeeded by the one shown in (C). It bears the same patent date and the caliber is marked in the same location. This one is "38" but few, if any, cartridges of this caliber used a Berdan primed cartridge. The finish is gold paint on the head and nickel plating

C

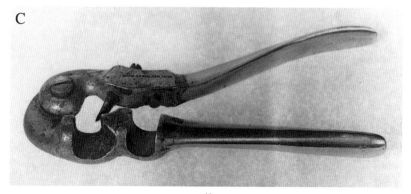

on the handles. The head portion is left rough to help the paint adhere. Berdan primers having largely vacated the American cartridge scene, the final tool in this series is a capper only. Its finish is the same gold and nickel as its immediate predecessor but at last the company stamped the caliber in a highly visible location, on the lower handle. One of these is shown in (D).

D

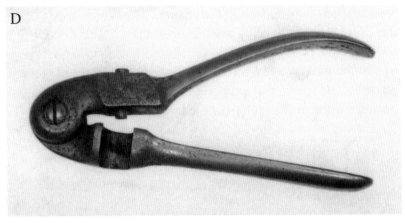

E

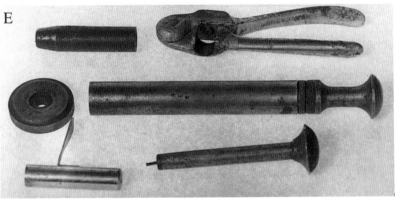

    A rather complete Remington reloading outfit is shown in (E). It accompanies an old bear hunter's Remington Hepburn sporting rifle chambered for the .40-3 1/4" Sharps cartridge. Since loads could vary even in the same caliber, many early cartridges were designated by their case length. As with many loading outfits, there is a wad cutter for cutting card wads to separate any lubricant used from the powder charge which would be quickly affected by it. To its right is the capper described above. Below it is the three-piece ball or bullet seater, the term "ball" being carried over from muzzle loading arms and still used in military parlance to differentiate regular cartridges from blanks. The leather spacers were not supplied by the factory but were added to regulate the bullet seating depth. No doubt in this case it was used to accommodate a maximum charge as this rifle was reportedly used to kill the last grizzly bear in California. Ball seaters are stamped on the side with the caliber. The base is used both in the decapping and bullet seating operations. The decapper is shown below it. A charge cup completes this outfit. The absence of a bullet mold may be attributed to the owner's use of factory-made bullets which were superior to most home cast bullets, especially when of the paper-patched type.

F

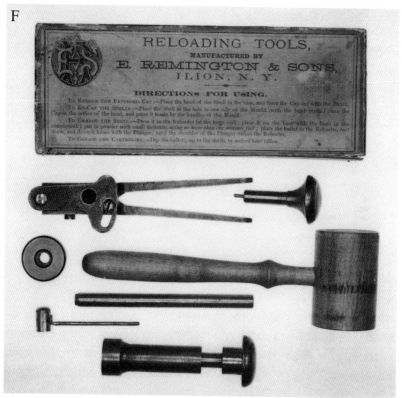

Remington made loading outfits for the smaller pistol-size cartridges as well. Shown here in (F) is one for the .32 Short, an early pistol size which could also be fired in some rifles. These small Remington bullet mold/cappers are nearly identical to the early ones made by Smith and Wesson but the handle ends are rounded like a Roman arch while the Smith and Wesson ones are more pointed like a Gothic arch. Also, at least in this example, they cap from the opposite direction. There are other minor differences which point to separate manufacturers but certainly some copying must have occurred by one or the other. The other items are similar to those in the larger reloading sets. The wooden mallet is used to drive the plunger down seating the bullet. The plain steel rod is apparently used to force the completed cartridge out of the ball seater as there is no other provision for doing so. Apparently these tools were furnished unfinished "in the white." Instructions are printed on the box cover and, this being an outside lubricated "heel" bullet, the user was told to "Dip the bullets, up to the shells, in melted beef tallow." None of the pieces of this set have any markings. The molds are very scarce and the other tools even more so.

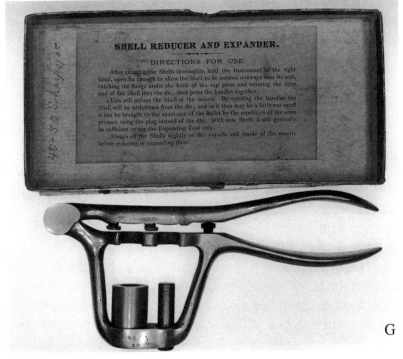

G

Remington called the special tool shown in (G) a "Shell Reducer and Expander" but the directions use the word "Instrument" perhaps in recognition of its fine construction and finish. They were not inexpensive being priced at $2.00 in the same catalog that listed the big rolling block No. 1 Sporting Rifle at $20.00 even in the large centerfire calibers like .45-70. They were not very popular judging by their scarcity today and were dropped from sale well before the turn of the century. Their sole purpose was to resize the mouths of cartridge cases and they are quite awkward to use because the shell must be angled into place and then aligned over either the reducer die or expander plug engaging a rigid rather than spring-loaded extractor hook. They are a reminder that some tools are scarce simply because they did not work well and accordingly were quickly discontinued. In this case the demise of the 1000 yard Creedmore style target shooting with its powerful cartridges may have played a part as well. The only marking is the caliber and it may be found outside the part housing the dies or on the top handle. The finish was either nickel plate or red paint. This specimen was housed in an absolutely plain red cardboard box with no label or other outside identification. The directions for use are inside the lid.

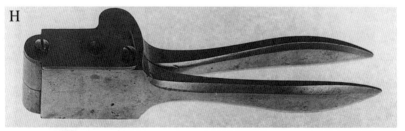

There are apparently only two types of Remington bullet molds other than the small mold/capper already described. The earliest of these is shown in (H). They are plain polished steel having distinctively-shaped handles and a bright blue sprue cutter. Only the caliber is marked on them, and it appears on the side of the block on the few specimens examined. This pattern was soon discontinued giving way to the more commonly seen (if that term can be used) kind shown in (I). The caliber may be found almost anywhere on the block portion or else on the sprue cutter. Sometimes it is just the bullet diameter such as "50," or may be more informative for example "44 S" for the .44-77

I

Sharps, " 40 310" indicating both caliber and weight, or even a rather complete "38-40-245," Remington's own straight-cased cartridge which should not be confused with the familiar .38-40 WCF. Thus we leave the Remington line of reloading tools and take up those by the Union Metallic Cartridge Company.

As its name implies, the Union Metallic Cartridge Company was in the business of manufacturing ammunition. Having begun in 1867 shortly after the Civil War ended, the term "metallic" had much significance. The war was fought largely with muzzle loaders using paper cartridges. Even the popular breech loading Sharps used a combustible cartridge. The effectiveness of fully self-contained metallic cartridges in Spencers and Henrys was amply demonstrated but not widely employed. Indeed

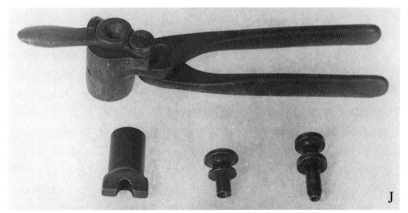

J

most civilian shooters fired muzzle loaders with loose powder and a cloth patched ball. U. M. C. Co. wisely assessed the future of the firearms market and went after the growing metallic cartridge trade, first with rimfires and then with centerfire, reloadable cartridges.

U. M. C. Co. seemingly marketed only one type of reloading outfit and it is shown in (J). Note that a means of

K

decapping and recapping is absent from the set. A U. M. C. Co. marked brass decapping rod is shown in (K). It is not known by the authors if it belonged to a set. The fact that all the other components are neatly marked with "U M C Co" suggests that a recapping tool similarly marked may sometime surface. A fair number of U. M. C. Co. molds are encountered though they must be considered scarce and the other tools rare. Much of the original red finish remains on this set. It is in "32 L. O." caliber, telling us that it is for the .32 Long Outside Lubricated cartridge— meaning that the lubricant covered the exposed portion of the bullet and not in grooves down inside the case mouth. The latter would be noted by the abbreviation "I. L." (inside lubricated).

The reloading process involved using the tapered plunger to expand the case mouth to admit the reduced diameter "heel" of the bullet. The other plunger is the bullet seater. The base is relieved on both sides to make removing the shell and then the finished cartridge easier. To date, the only other U. M. C. tool examined was the body and seating plunger of one made for a .22 caliber cartridge. It was identical in design but somewhat smaller. Whether it was for the .22 Maynard or even for loading the primed empty .22 rimfire shells once available is not known.

U. M. C. molds are customarily marked on the base with the company initials and the caliber. They were made in many calibers up to at least .50-90 Sharps paper patched and .50-115 Bullard. It may be that many were sold separately from the tools thus accounting for the greater number seen today as compared to U. M. C. tools.

The best source of published information on the Bridgeport Gun Implement Company products is a reprint of its 1882 catalog in the May 1966 issue of the *Canadian Journal of Arms Collecting*. While most of their tools are for shotguns and are thus outside the scope of this study, they did make some tools for reloading rifle and pistol cartridges. The B. G. I. catalog listed

L

two complete reloading sets. The basic economy set sold for $2.00 to $3.00 each at the per dozen price depending on caliber. This set, catalog number 1200, appears to have been limited to pistol-size cartridges. A complete set is shown in (L). The cylindrical object is the body or barrel of the ball seater while its seating plunger is on the right. The plunger decapper is on the left. Also shown are the decapping base, powder dipper, and the odd, hook-type capper reminiscent of those found on the end of one style of Colt bullet mold. The mold here is painted red though black ones are seen. On the cutoff plate is "38 S & W" and "B. G. I. Co." For larger cartridges there were sturdier sets. They had a better quality, tong-type capper, mallet, wad cutter, and a strange "screw shell crimper" which could also be purchased separately. These sets sold for $5.50 and $6.00 again depending on caliber. They could even furnish a set of "Sharps Regular Reloading Tools" for a little more. We do know that the Sharps Rifle Co. sold mold-making tools and marking dies to the B. G. I. Co. in 1881 and B. G. I. apparently continued to sell this type of mold after Sharps had ceased operation. A B. G. I. Co. mold

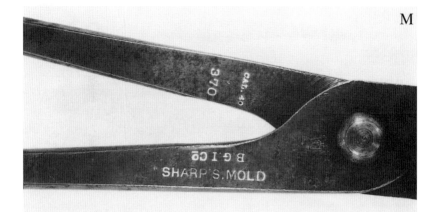

marked "Sharp's Mold", "B. G. I. Co.", "Cal 40", and "370" (the bullet weight) is shown in (M). It is a typical Sharps mold in every respect except markings. Note the incorrect apostrophe in the Sharps name. Cartridge boxes are sometimes similarly mislabeled.

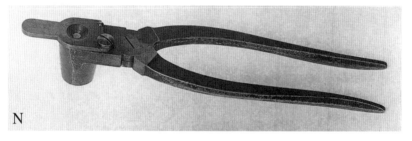

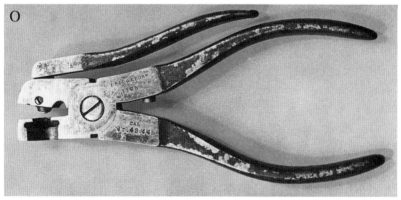

A type of mold illustrated in the B. G. I. catalog but marked "S. D. & G" is shown in (N). The initials stand for the New York firm of Schoeverling, Daly, and Gales. It is also marked "38 ev'l"

indicating use in some sort of everlasting cartridge, probably Ballard's .38-50. Its finish is red paint on the handles with shiny mold blocks.

B. G. I. made a peculiar three-handled tool with the same finish as the mold just described. It was designed for use with Berdan primers. The shell was put in place and the large handles closed. By rotating the small handle, a small chisel emerged to pry out the fired primer. By using only the large handles, a new primer could be seated. Unlike its other products, this one carries its catalog number of 1185. A specimen of this tool, made for .42, .43, and .44 calibers, all having the same head size, is shown in (O).

By specializing in gun implements, the B. G. I. Co. could well be the source of tools and molds sold by other companies; for example, the Marlin marked Sharps mold.

IV

MARLIN, BALLARD, AND BROWNING

The names Marlin and Ballard are inextricably connected in the arms field. In fact, until a few decades ago Marlin advertisements spoke with pride of their Ballard-type rifling to which they attributed great accuracy. Rifles were manufactured on the Ballard patent by a series of companies but it was the later ones, those made by J. M. Marlin and then the Marlin Firearms Company, that achieved great fame on target ranges and in the field. They were chambered for a variety of centerfire, reloadable cartridges; and tools were designed especially for them. The John Browning connection is through his design of the 1881 Marlin loading tool.

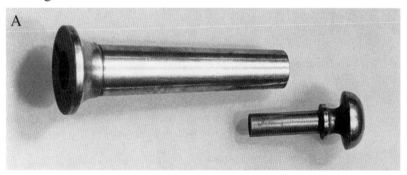

A

Ballard rifles, being single-shots, did not need crimped cartridges. Indeed, uncrimped cases lasted longer and would not damage the paper patched bullets common in the 1870's and 1880's. Thus the basic loading tool was a straight-line bullet seater. One such Ballard seater is shown in (A). The caliber marking is found on the top of the plunger or on the base of the tool. To use it the bullet was carefully started into the charged case by hand to reduce the chance of tearing the patch. It was then inserted into the body of the tool, the latter placed on a flat surface, and the plunger pushed down to seat the bullet. There is a groove in the base to facilitate the removal of the loaded cartridge. The tool is nickel plated. Its only marking is its caliber.

Decapping and recapping were accomplished using the distinctive tool shown in (B). This tool was produced in a range of sizes and marked only with the caliber. The decapping pin protruded from one handle and was protected by a knurled, screw-on cap. With the old-style soft primers a hard push, or at most a light mallet tap, would drive out the fired primer. Like the seater this implement was also finished in nickel plate. The rest of the standard loading kit consisted of a powder scoop, wad cutter, and bullet mold. An optional accessory was a bullet swage to more accurately form the cast bullets and a case sizer. The former was used primarily by target shooters. Still another optional item was called the "Wilkinson Loader." The metering portion of one is shown in (C). It is calibrated in grains and drams of powder as well as ounces of shot. Stamped on the top is "J. D. Wilkinson, Plattsburg, N. Y. Pat'd July 24, 1877." It is a rare item.

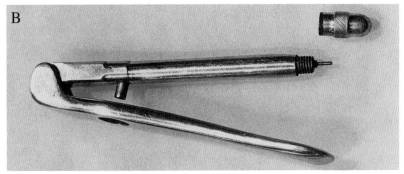

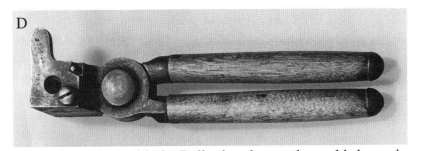

D

Furnished with the Ballard tools was the mold shown in (D). It bears the Marlin Firearms Company initials "M. F. A. Co." on the cutoff plate indicating production after 1881. Prior to this time the company had been J. M. Marlin. It bears a great similarity to Ideal molds but is quickly distinguished by the neat metal endcaps on the handles. Reportedly some very early Ideal molds were so made. An early brass Marlin bullet mold is shown in (E). It is not known what the very earliest Marlin molds looked like—those made during the J. M. Marlin period. Perhaps Marlin simply bought them on the open market or else did not mark them.

E

The molds illustrated are not the only Marlin-marked molds. The subject was extensively explored in "Marlin Bullet Molds" in the November 1994 issue of *The Gun Report*. The relatively scarce Marlin mold shown in (F) is found in both grooved and patched varieties. It is immediately distinguishable by the "bow-legged" shape of its handles, note the similarity to the B. G. I. Co. molds. Known specimens carry the "M. F. A. Co." stamp as well as the caliber on the cutoff. The company placed orders with outside suppliers as well. Early type iron handled Winchester molds are found occasionally with the familiar "M. F. A. Co." stamp but not the customary Winchester markings. One, not marked with either name, bears "40-M" on

F

the handle. Its cavity is for the distinctive Marlin bullet shape having a flatter nose than Winchester bullets. Sometimes the familiar Sharps bullet mold with its distinctive sprue nippers on the end is found marked "M. F. A. Co." These may well have been made by the Bridgeport Gun Implement Company which reportedly made them for Sharps.

G

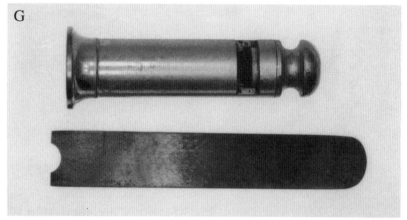

When Marlin began manufacturing a repeating rifle, their first attempt at a loading tool was the one shown in (G). Note how similar the conformation is to that of the Ballard seater. It too was nickel plated. Its use differed in that the assembled cartridge was placed into the top and the very short plunger driven down to crimp the bullet in place. Extraction of the completed cartridge was with a plain, blued flat piece of steel having a curved end to engage the cartridge at its rim through the opening shown. These tools are quite scarce and the extractors almost never found. Extractors are unmarked and would be a candidate for the scrap pile of the unknowing. The tool is marked with caliber only.

Now it is time to take up a splendid example of the machinist's art, the successor to the tool just described, called "handsome" in the December 1986 issue of *The Gun Report*. The Marlin company must have been proud of them as they are serially numbered. We speak here of the Model 1881 combination loading tool and bullet mold. It is shown in (H). But before examining it in detail, the story behind it should be understood. That story is nicely explained and the record set straight in "The Browning Bros. Loading Tools" by Art Gogan and Fred Selman in the November-December 1993 issue of *Man at Arms*. The Browning Bros. referred to was the Ogden, Utah Territory firm of which John M. Browning was to have such a momentous impact upon the Winchester Repeating Arms Company and indeed the whole field of firearms design.

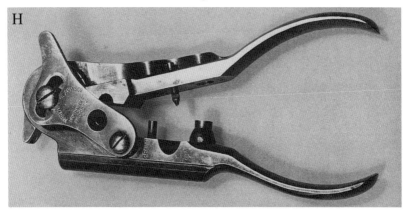

H

The Brownings were manufacturing a combination reloading tool and bullet mold mostly for the local trade. Winchester contended that it infringed on their V. A. King patent No. 232189 of September 14, 1880 (see patent in Appendix) and insisted that production and sale of them cease. Browning's first model loading tool followed exactly its patent No. 247881 dated October 4, 1881. This tool is shown in (I). They are generally stamped "J. M. Browning, Ogden, UT" followed by the caliber and are a scarce tool as are all Browning tools. Based on their research Gogan and Selman contend, quite convincingly, that this is *not* the loading tool in question as the patent was almost immediately assigned to the Marlin Firearms Company. Indeed some are found marked with the Marlin stamp. The controversial tool is apparently that shown in (J). Most of these bear no marking at

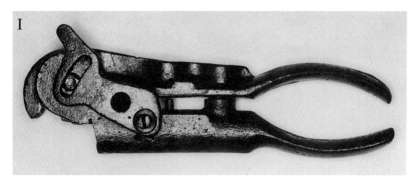

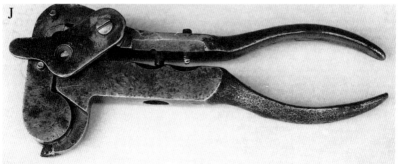

all except the caliber. They were made in three sizes. The one seen here is for a long straight .45 caliber cartridge, perhaps the Sharps .45-2.4" though it will accept the full length 2 7/8" case. Unlike some specimens it is equipped with a Berdan decapping chisel. Its location has been moved resulting in defacing of the caliber marking. With production of this tool stopped by Winchester, a third tool was designed and manufactured by the Brownings. It is shown in (K). Its seating die is detachable, merely sitting in a hole in the handle of the tool. The completed cartridge was pried from the die with the clawed end of one handle. This awkward method was necessary so as not to infringe upon the King patent.

Meanwhile, the Marlin Firearms Company had put the 1881 tool into production. These beautifully machined tools were highly polished and carry a fine blued finish. They are relatively scarce. The number produced may be deduced from the serial numbers reported which exceed 7600. The mold cavity is contained inside the tool near the hinge and the "ear" of its sprue cutter plate serves as a scraper to clean out case mouths and re-

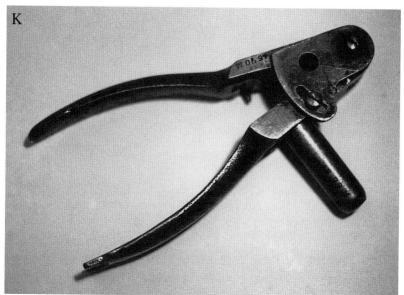

store them to roundness. See close-up (L). An unusual feature of this tool is the incorporation of a wad cutter. It is located adjacent to the capping hole and its sharp edges and close fit assure excellent wads. Decapping was usually with a decapping pin or "plug" but Berdan shells could be decapped with the adjustable chisel. The assembled cartridge was placed in the chamber inside one handle and the handles opened to seat and crimp the bullet in place. Closing them withdrew it. An instruction

L

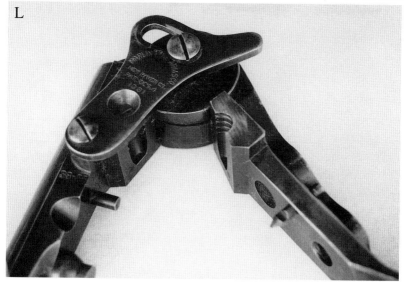

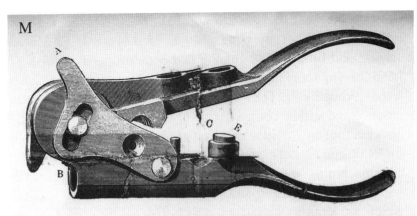

MARLIN LOADER.

This tool is the *only* compete one made. It combines in one piece an entire reloading outfit consisting of Bullet Mould, Wad Cutter, Decapper, Recapper and Crimper. No other make of tool has the Bullet Mould and Wad Cuttr. Although providing for all these necessary functions and rendering double the service of any other tool on the market, it is very compact and in weight much less than others.

If the mouth of the shell, after firing, should be dented or out of shape, it can be rounded out on the shell scraper at *A*.

For removing the primer from a shell which has only one vent, use the decapper plug at *B* ; if several vents, use the pin at *C*.

To recap the shell, insert same at *D*, and after placing the primer in its pocket, bring the handles of the tool together.

E is the Wad Cutter, which will do the work with less trouble and more perfectly than an ordinary tool for that special purpose.

Be careful to recap the shell while empty, which will avoid dangerous explosions. Then insert the powder, wad and ball, after lubricating the latter, into the shell and place it in the chamber at *B*. By drawing the handles apart the shell is crimped and the ball firmly seated. Bring the handles together again and the finished cartridge will be lifted from the chamber.

Do not use powder which is finer than F. G., and by all means avoid the high grades, such as Electric, Diamond Grain, &c.

Always keep your mould and lead very hot while using, as otherwise a perfect ball cannot be produced.

THE MARLIN FIRE ARMS CO.,

MANUFACTURERS,

New Haven, Conn.

sheet for the 1881 tool is shown in (M). These tools were made for a short time. They were not yet listed in the 1882 Marlin catalog and by the 1888 catalog had been dropped in favor of Ideal loading tools though the Ballard tools continued to be offered. Probably the 1881 Marlin tool was just too expensive to produce and still be competitively priced. When the Ideal combination tool and mold was priced at $3.00, the Marlin tool sold for $4.00 and almost certainly lost money at that with all its intricate machining and elaborate finishing. Thus passed from the scene a beautiful implement for a rather mundane task but one which modern-day collectors can cherish as an artifact of another era.

N

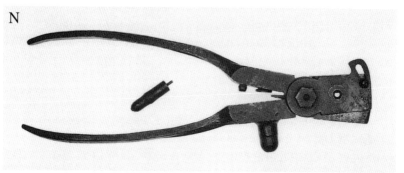

Before leaving the subject of Browning loading tools, a completely unmarked tool/mold is shown in (N) which may have some association with them. It is for a .38 caliber pistol cartridge. There is a small extractor next to the seating orifice to withdraw the loaded cartridge. Interestingly, it has a movable brass "pressing block' like that covered in the King/Winchester patent of 1880 to allow the cartridge to be pressed straight down into the seating chamber. It is peened in place. This entire tool has a frontier gunsmith look about it but may have been in very limited production.

Mention should be made of tools and molds made during the time Ideal Manufacturing Company was owned by Marlin. They are the regular Ideal line and are covered in the Ideal chapter.

V

MAYNARD AND STEVENS

By profession, Dr. Edward Maynard was a dentist; but gun collectors know him best for a whole series of firearms innovations. Indeed, Frank Sellers in his *American Gunsmiths* lists 22 different gun-related patents issued to him. Maynard is probably best known for his tape priming system which used a roll of paper caps much like those used in toy cap pistols. It was a feature of some U. S. long arms. The other is for the Civil War carbine which bears his name. There was, in fact, briefly a Maynard Arms Company created to market what collectors know as the First Model Maynard. However, actual manufacture was by the Massachusetts Arms Company. Soon the Maynard Company name was dropped but the products of his inventiveness continued to be made by the Massachusetts Arms Company. Ultimately, in 1891, that company was absorbed by the J. Stevens Arms and Tool Company. Due to their close association, the products of these companies will be considered together.

Before examining the Maynard reloading implements, it may be useful to recall that there were three distinct lines of cartridges used in Maynard rifles. The first became known as the Model 1865 and is familiar to many collectors through the fairly common .50 caliber Civil War carbine cartridge having a very large diameter but thin rim with a central hole to convey the flash from the external percussion cap. Less commonly seen in this series are the .35, .40, and shotshell versions. Following them came the completely self-contained Model 1873 with its large, thick rim and Berdan primer. Finally, the Model 1882 cartridges appeared which were conventional in appearance.

A typical Maynard bullet mold is shown in (A). They are customarily marked "Manufactured by Mass. Arms Co., Chicopee Falls." The very earliest ones also bear the Maynard Arms Company stamp and cast a distinctive pointed bullet. Two cavities are standard on the later ones but single cavities are equally rep-

A

resented in the scarce Maynard Arms Co. products. Often they will cast bullets of differing design though of the same caliber. See (B) There is a "1," "2," or "3" stamped outside the cavity to identify the bullet shape. Number 1 has a conical shape, number 2 is more cylindrical, and number 3 is a very long cylindrical bullet. The number 3 cavities are seldom encountered. Maynard sporting rifles often had two or more interchangeable barrels all of different calibers so some molds cast two different caliber bullets. A small hole in the hinge, not seen on the earliest molds, is for lubricant to keep the close fitting halves working smoothly. In later years, Harry Pope's molds had a similar feature. Maynard molds were of polished steel. Those for the Civil War Smith carbine are similar but have a single large cavity.

B

All Maynard molds are relatively scarce, but the one shown in (C) is a rare variation indeed. It is discussed in detail in the August 1988 issue of *The Gun Report*. Basically it is a regular two-cavity mold but has a plate permanently attached to the bottom into which hollow pointing plugs fit. Note the extreme depth of the cavity. A .22 blank or short cartridge just exactly fits the cavity with its base flush; the rim fitting into a recess formed by a shoulder on the plug. This .40 caliber mold was a factory product advertised along with molds for .44 and .50 caliber.

C

Another rare variation that is not shown is also a two-cavity mold. The cavity closest to the hinge pin casts a Number 1 style conical-shaped bullet. The second cavity casts a separate tip bullet. The Ideal Manufacturing Company would later utilize this concept which is explained in detail in the Ideal chapter.

What apparently is a late Maynard or early Stevens mold is shown in (D). These quite scarce molds are entirely different from the usual Maynard mold but are found in the distinctive Maynard (and later Stevens) calibers. Jim Grant, in his *Single Shot Rifles* attributes them to Maynard, but one has been reported marked Stevens. Most have a single cavity but one, in .22 caliber, has two. There are usually no markings. The finish is rough unlike any other Maynard product. They are a mystery that awaits further identification.

D

Very much like the standard Maynard in appearance is this early Stevens mold shown with its accompanying ball seater in (E). It was the subject of a June 1997 article in *The Gun Report*. They are very scarce. The only marking is "J. Stevens & Co" on the handle. It appears to be a copy of the Maynard rather than just differently marked because there are distinct differences.

E

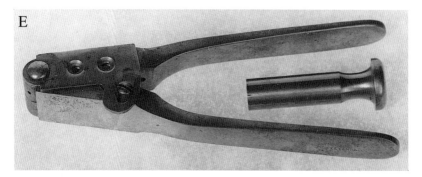

Most noticeable is that the sprue plate cuts from the opposite side. Less obvious is that the handles are slightly shorter and thicker than on its Maynard counterpart. Since the company name changed to J. Stevens Arms and Tool Co. after 1880, this mold must precede that date. Like the Maynard it was produced with a polished steel finish.

Turning to the Maynard tools, we show in (F) those used in reloading the thick rim, Berdan primed 1873 cartridge. The head of a cartridge protrudes from the ball seater shown with its wooden base. A special capper to accommodate the large rim is shown at the left. Primers are removed with the Hadley's "cap picker" at the far right. A small chisel can be made to protrude from its face to pierce and remove the fired primer. With their

F

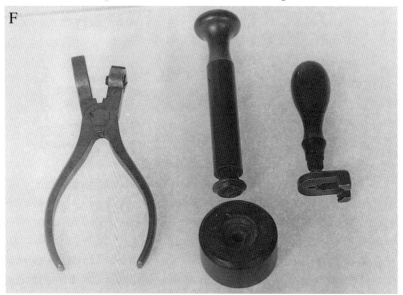

large diameter rims, the Model 1865 and 1873 cartridges were fairly easy to withdraw by hand; but the 1882 cartridges required that the lower end of the ball seater be relieved to offer a better grip, as shown in (G). An 1873 style seater is shown above it. The very earliest Maynard ball seaters had a vent hole in the side below the knob. In later ones it was centered in the top. A surprising amount of information is found on the top of these seaters suggesting that they were made to order. The early one shown has "40 1 70 G" one above the other indicating .40 caliber, loading the number 1 bullet with 70 grains of powder. The later 1882 seater has "32 P 35 G" referring to the .32-35 Maynard cartridge using a patched bullet. Unaccountably there is an "N" at one side suggesting that it could seat "naked"; that is, unpatched bullets as well. The 1865 cartridges, having an external ignition source, required no decapping or recapping tools. One wonders how many of these and other scarce tools may have been discarded because their identity and purpose was unknown.

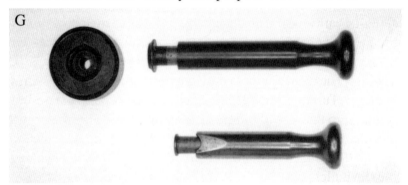

The 1882 Maynard cartridges could be decapped from within and Mr. Hadley obliged with the ingenious tool shown in (H) accompanied by its cardboard box. The fired case was placed on the rod or mandrel and one handle raised causing the pin to push out the primer. With the case still in place, a fresh primer was started in its pocket and the other handle was raised which seated it. Both handles are spring loaded to return them to a horizontal position. The body of the tool is generally gold painted with handles of black wood. The tool shown is nickel-plated with black wooden handles. A patent date of "JAN. 13, 1885" is

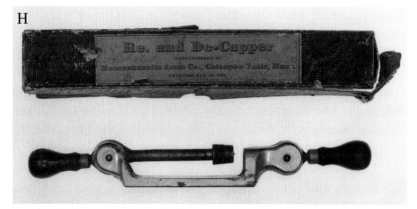

generally found stamped either on the base of the tool under a coat of gold paint or along the length of the mandrel. A patent drawing of this interesting tool is included in the appendix. Those Hadley re/decappers observed to date have had a serial number stamped on them ranging to over 400.

A simple, unmarked but rare Maynard "screw loader" is shown in (I). This plain tool was utilized with Maynard's 1882 series of cartridges. The decapping rod was pushed down inside the cartridge case to deprime it. The deprimed case was then placed in a die (not shown) that would also be used for bullet seating. The die was grooved to fit over an opening in the "screw loader." Turning the winged screw against a plate pressed the primer into the base of the case repriming it. Finally, the primed and charged case was again placed in the die along with the bullet and the winged screw was again turned against the plate seating the bullet.

I

A rare Maynard bullet lubricator pump is shown in (J). It has no markings but is identified from an illustration in A. C. Gould's *Modern American Rifles* published in 1892. This specimen differs only in having a plain plunger instead of a winged screw to exert pressure on the lubricant. The bullet is placed in the hole and the plunger pressed forcing lubricant into the bullet's solitary lubricating groove.

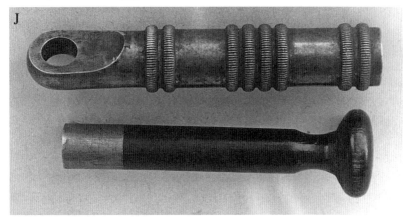

Before leaving Maynard and Stevens, we should acknowledge an Ideal tool specifically made for Stevens and its cartridges. The largest of the Ideal tong tools were designated No. 6. This tool shown in (K) is listed as the No. 6-A and was made almost exclusively for the .32-35, .38-35, and .38-45 Stevens everlasting cartridges. Its most distinguishing feature is a sprue cutter which swings opposite to those on other Ideal tools. Also the plate may say "For Stevens Arms Co. Chicopee Falls." This is another scarce one.

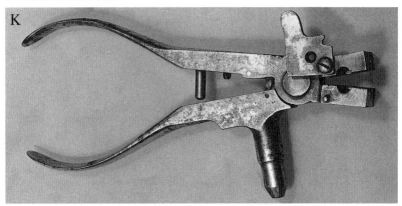

Finally, for a few years Stevens employed Harry Pope to oversee the manufacture of his line of tools as well as the rifling of his special barrels. That topic is dealt with in another chapter.

VI

WHITNEY

One of the most interesting of all American arms companies is that begun by Eli Whitney. Though much better known by the general public as the inventor of the cotton gin, this device was easily and widely copied and he failed to profit very much from it. With no experience in the manufacture of firearms, he nevertheless was able to secure a contract in 1798 for 10,000 muskets from the U.S. Government and thus embarked in an arms business that was to last well beyond his lifetime, indeed until bought out by Winchester in the 1880's.

This company, which styled itself Whitneyville Armory and later Whitney Arms Company, produced a great variety of arms during almost a century in business including a large order for Model 1841 "Mississippi" rifles and the famous Colt Walker revolvers. In addition, it made a significant contribution to the concept of interchangeable parts and mass production. Since our focus here is on cartridge reloading tools, we must look at the last few years of the company's existence. This period saw the production of a series of breech loading repeaters on Burgess, Kennedy, and Scharf patents, single shot rolling blocks patterned after Remington's, and the unusual Phoenix and Howard "Thunderbolt." Whitney does not seem to have developed a distinctive cartridge of its own. Their rolling blocks and Phoenix rifles were available for almost every popular caliber.

It appears that Whitney made only one basic set of loading tools and they are rarely, if ever, marked with the company's name. Catalog illustrations have been the principal means of identifying them. Reproduced here is a page from the Whitney catalog for 1884 showing them.(A).

A set of tools usually sold for $5.00. There was an extra charge for the express cartridge set made especially for loading the .50-95 Winchester cartridge with its hollow point bullet for which some of Whitney's repeaters were chambered. The tools could also be purchased individually at $1.00 for the cap extrac-

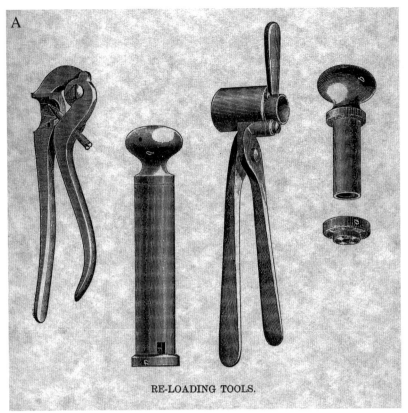

A

RE-LOADING TOOLS.

tor, $2.75 for the ball seater, and $1.25 for the bullet mold. These are the three items illustrated. While called a "cap extractor" this tool would also reportedly recap the shell. Supposedly this was done by turning the upper handle around so that a small lump would bear down on the new primer thus seating it. However efforts to seat primers in this fashion have been unsuccessful, so the means of capping is still unknown. A Whitney cap extractor is shown in (B).

Whitney ball seaters were of two kinds. One is of three-piece construction with a mushroom top on the seating plunger. A small notch in the base permits extraction of the completed cartridge. What looks like another tool and base in the catalog illustration are merely duplications of the plunger and base, perhaps because they are partially concealed in the assembled tool in the illustration. A specimen of this tool is shown in (C). It is marked only with the caliber. The design is typical of the non-

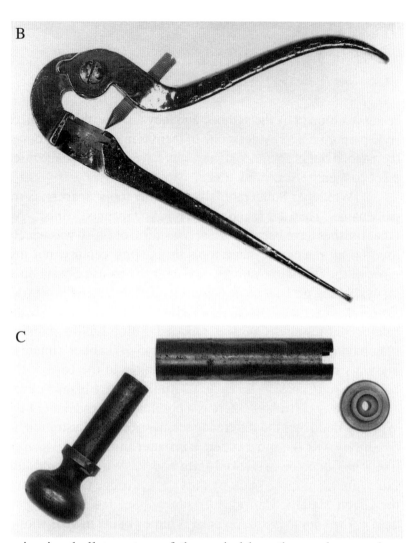

B

C

crimping bullet seaters of the period by other makers such as Ballard and Remington. Although the plunger seems unduly long it is correct.

The other seater is of a two-piece design: a base like the one in the catalog illustration and a body. It is probable that this design came about from the desire to crimp some cartridges. The one shown in (D) is marked with the caliber .50-70 and there is a small "G" after it to indicate that it is for grooved bullets, which are crimped, as opposed to patched ones which are not. There would have been no need for the plunger. Of those Whitney ball

D

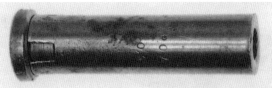

seaters examined by the authors, and they are few, this two-piece style predominates. At least one of them is made for a customarily patched bullet so the company may have abandoned the three piece tool entirely at some time.

Whitney's bullet mold, like its other tools, bears no company name. They are found with a black "Japanned" finish. No other finishes have been reported. This form of finish was widely used on all manner of hand tools in the 19th century, not just those of the reloading variety. The caliber was usually stamped on the bottom of the mold blocks as well as the intended powder charge, for example, "44 CAL 77 GR." Those seen are like the catalog illustration. One was reported with a hollow pointing plug having a wooden handle. It is in .45-70 caliber. Interestingly, its cavity is very deep, in fact almost to the base of the bullet. It is of a size to accept a .22 rimfire, either blank or even a loaded long cartridge. There is a possible minor variant of the Whitney mold and the difference seems, from an illustration, to be entirely with the sprue cutter. It is flatter and the end is shaped like a half octagon as viewed from above. Whitney molds are fairly similar to those made by the U.S. Cartridge Company and the Union Metallic Cartridge Company. See the July 1990 article in *The Gun Report*. A typical Whitney bullet mold is shown in (E).

When Winchester absorbed the financially ailing Whitney Arms Company in 1888, no attempt was made to continue with any of the Whitney products.

E

VII

SHARPS

Other than Winchester and Colt no name looms larger among American gunmakers of the 19th century than Sharps. Known as "Beecher's Bibles" and the chosen weapon of John Brown, as the choice of Berdan's Sharpshooters and a cavalry favorite, as the premier tool of the professional buffalo hunters in the West, and on the 1000 yard Creedmoor ranges, the Sharps has earned a special place in our history. For purposes of this study, our focus is on the period beginning in the late 1860's and ending when production ceased in 1881 during which time the company made reloading implements for fully self-contained cartridges.

Frank Sellers devotes an entire chapter to Sharps loading tools in his definitive *Sharps Firearms* with much detail and an abundance of photographs including the pre-metallic cartridge era. Readers are directed to this excellent resource for information not found here which of necessity is a sampling.

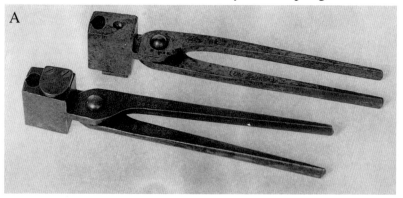

Fortunately Sharps molds usually carry quite a bit of information. Two typical ones are shown in (A). Their most obvious feature is the distinctive nippers on the end which are used to remove the sprue left over from casting the bullet. Appearing on the handle of one mold in brackets is "Old Reliable" a trademark added to Sharps rifles in 1876 and presumably to the molds about the same time. Also on the handles is a number which is apparently a factory assembly number which would keep the two parts together until final assembly. On the underside is "Cal 40" and "330" representing the caliber and bullet weight. Also on the handle is "Sharps Rifle Co., Bridgeport, Conn." The other mold is virtually identical but serves to illustrate the underside with its plate which closes the base of the cavity and has a convex protrusion which forms a dished base on the bullet. After the paper patch is wrapped around the bullet, the end of the paper is twisted into a "tail" and pressed into the recess to help hold the patch in place in the loading process. The second mold is an earlier one and does not have the "Old Reliable" stamp though it does have the company name and Bridgeport address. It is marked "Cal 45" followed by "1 1/10 indicating bullet *length* and "420" its weight. This bullet was standard in the Sharps version of the .45-70. It should be noted that the same kind of mold is seen with Marlin and Bridgeport Gun Implement Company markings. They are discussed elsewhere. A rare variation of the Sharps mold is shown in (B). It casts a grooved bullet and has a sprue cutoff, both unusual features.

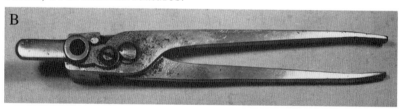

A far less common type of Sharps mold is shown in (C). A side view is shown in (D). It is of brass with a steel cutoff plate. On the tang is "Sharps Rifle Co." The caliber appears on the plate; in this instance, .44 caliber weighing 520 grains. This long, very heavy bullet was used in the 2 5/8 inch case propelled by as much as 105 grains of powder for 1000 yard Creedmoor target shooting. These brass molds apparently cast bullets that were to be swaged before use but in later days were simply offered as a cheap mold for bullets to be fired as cast. These appear to be identical to the first type Winchester molds.

Shown in (E) are several Sharps reloading implements. The upper left item is a bullet or ball seater of the earlier type. A

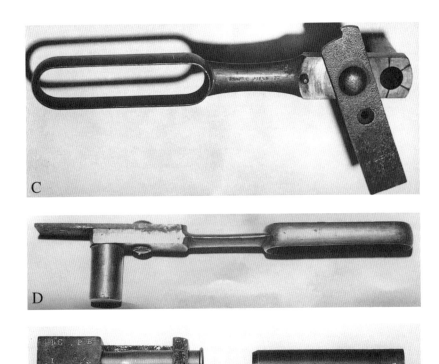

cartridge case has been inserted to show how it is used. It carries the small "Sharps Rifle Co." stamp plus "44 C P B 1 1/4 I N" indicating that it is for seating a .44 caliber patched bullet of 1 1/4 inch in length. More often seen is the one at the top right. Also a one-piece tool it has the caliber on the side near the top. This one is marked "45 420 2 1/10" showing the caliber, bullet weight, and case length. This information may be found on the top of the seater instead of the side. As with most such seaters the sole function is to keep the bullet in alignment as it is pushed into place so as not to damage the patch. Like most other seaters these do not crimp the case mouth.

On the lower left is a Sharps wad cutter which carries the

company name and caliber. Paper patched bullets were dry and some shooters liked to use a lubricating wad behind them. To protect the powder from the effects of the moist lubricant, a wad was placed on top of the powder. The object on the lower right is what Sharps called a "follower," actually a wad seater. These are often marked with the company name on the top or the side. One is seen in (F). They also had an additional purpose: A thin layer of lubricant was spread on the wad mold and, when cool, was pressed out by the follower.

F

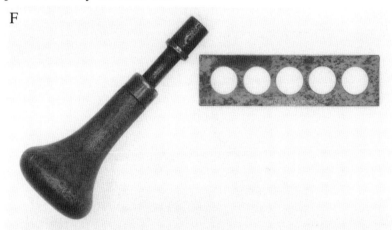

The fired Berdan primer was pried out with a simple awl having a handle like that of the follower.

The Sharps powder dipper was of a distinctive style. One is shown in (G). While they usually bore the familiar small company stamp, this one does not. Its only marking is the powder charge on the bottom, in this case "50," which would have to be for the only Sharps cartridge using this comparatively small charge, the .40-50 either bottlenecked or straight.

Earlier reference was made to bullet swaging. Most hunters did not bother to perform this operation; but many target shooters, seeking the best in accuracy, did. The cast bullet was placed

G

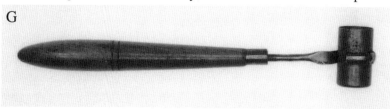

in the body of the swage and actually pounded to insure maximum density and uniformity of each bullet. Shown in (H) is one for the .40-330 bullet of 1 1/8th inch length.

Also in the Sharps line was the case sizer. This one (I) is in .45-2 7/8 inch size and was used to reduce oversize cases. The long plunger expanded the case mouth to the correct size, a crucial matter when loading paper patched bullets.

VIII

SMITH AND WESSON

The purpose of cartridge reloading implements is to cast bullets and/or load ammunition in a proper and expeditious way. The esthetics of loading tools was generally of little consequence in the past just as it is today. But if any reloading implement can be called "beautiful," it has to be the later model combination bullet mold and capper made by Smith and Wesson. Before continuing with the subject, some background on the company is appropriate.

Smith and Wesson is an old company dating back to 1852. Its earliest products were the Volcanic arms which fired a bullet propelled by a priming charge contained in its hollow base. There was no cartridge case. While an unsuccessful design, it was a repeater and its tubular magazine mechanism became the basis for the famous Henry and the earliest Winchester repeating rifles.

Very soon after the Volcanics came the .22 caliber rimfire revolver which, with its successors, was to give Smith and Wesson a significant role in firearms history. Our interest, focused on reloading tools, begins in the early 1870's when their line began to include revolvers firing reloadable centerfire ammunition.

Excellent research articles on the Smith and Wesson reloading tools and molds by Richard R. Bennett appeared in the 1980's issues of *Collector News,* the official publication of the Smith and Wesson Collectors Association. We have drawn extensively from them. The fact that none of the company's loading implements were marked complicates their identification, but their distinctive configuration helps greatly as does the lucky occurrence of finding them in factory boxed sets. Apparently production began in 1874, soon after the Smith and Wesson centerfire revolvers reached the market and continued to 1912. Unlike some other companies, they made tools only for their own firearms. All of their tools are scarce and a few downright rare.

The most conspicuous of the loading items, and the most likely to be encountered, are the bullet molds. Their change in style can be fairly well dated. All were equipped with a primer seater or capper. The capper could be adjusted to control the depth that the primer was seated. Opposite it was a hole to hold the shell while being primed. The earlier molds were made entirely of iron. The very earliest of these had a latch to hold the handles together while casting bullets. They were in production from 1874 to 1879. See (A). Apparently the latch was not very useful, and by 1880 the mold underwent a design change eliminating the latch and reversing the position of the primer seater and shell hole. These molds are nearly identical to ones made by Remington but differ in having somewhat pointed handle ends and in other minor particulars suggesting that they were made by different companies. An early set is shown in (B). Note the instructions were on the lid. (C)

A

Beginning in 1889, the last type of mold was offered; and it continued in production until 1912. It is this last mold that deserves to be called "beautiful." Most noteworthy are the handles which are of handsomely sculpted and finished hardwood in what has been called "peanut" shape. Rather than the plain unfinished surface of the earlier molds, these are highly polished and blued. The single cavity had given way to two cavities, typically one regular and one round ball. The round ball enabled the reloader to make up "gallery" loads using light charges for the indoor target shooting which had become popular. The bullet cavities

B

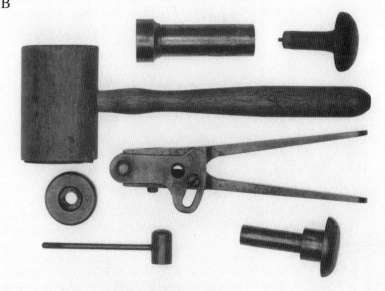

C

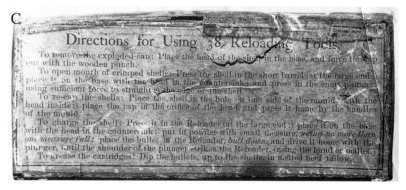

Directions for Using 38 Reloading Tools.

To remove the exploded cap: Place the head of the shell in the base, and force the cap out with the wooden punch.

To open mouth of crimped shells: Press the shell in the short barrel (at the large end) place it on the base with the head in the countersink; and press in the short plunger using sufficient force to straighten the edge of the shell.

To re-cap the shells: Place the shell in the hole on one side of the mould with the head inside; place the cap in the orifice of the head, and press it home by the handles of the mould.

To charge the shell: Press it in the Reloader (at the large end,) place it on the base with the head in the countersink; put in powder with small measure, using no more than one measure full; place the bullet in the Reloader, butt down, and drive it home with the plunger, until the shoulder of the plunger strikes the Reloader, (using the hand or mallet.)

To grease the cartridges: Dip the bullets, up to the shells, in melted beef tallow.

had been moved out beyond the hinge and the capper was located next to the handle. Some variations exist such as molds casting only round balls and even a four-cavity version with two cutoff plates, one on the top and the other on the bottom.

The other components of Smith and Wesson loading sets can be very puzzling but consist of an array of plungers and dies and a circular base for the operations of decapping, crimp removal, and bullet seating plus a decapping pin. The earliest decappers were of wood and had a broad mushroom head. Later sets have a simple knock-out pin. One to four powder dippers were furnished—each stamped with its charge in grains. Some later plungers were knurled and others casehardened in color. All are finely fit and finished. A set is shown in (D). Instructions were printed inside the lid. Those from a Smith and Wesson catalog are shown in (E).

D

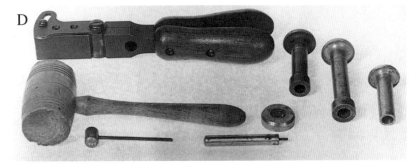

E Directions for the Use of Reloading Tools.

To Remove the Exploded Cap.--Place the head of the shell in the base, and force the cap out with the punch

To Open the Mouth of Crimped Shells.—Press the shell in the short barrel (at the large end), place it on the base with the head in the countersink, and push in the short plunger, using sufficient force to straighten the edge of the shell.

To Re-Cap the Shells.—Place the shell in the hole on one side of the mould (with the head inside), place the cap in the orifice of the head, and press it home by the handles of the mould.

To Cast the Bullets.—Use one ounce of tin to one pound of lead. Keep the moulds tightly closed when running the metal, as otherwise the bullet will be cast too large and will not enter the shell.

To Charge the Shell.—Press it in the reloader (at the large end); place it on the base with the head in the countersink; put in powder with the measure, using no more than one measure full; place the bullet in the reloader, butt down, and drive it home with the plunger until the shoulder of the plunger strikes the reloader (using the mallet or hand).

To Crimp the Shells Loaded with Conical Bullets.—Place the head of the cartridge in the countersink in the base, and drive the crimper over it until the end of the crimper meets the base.

N. B.—The groove in conical bullets must be perfectly filled with tallow before loading.

The cartridges loaded with round balls must be greased by dropping one drop of melted beef tallow into the shell above the ball.

The company chambered some of its revolvers for the .44-40 and .32-20 cartridges and recommended the reloader use Winchester tools for reloading these calibers, perhaps because their slightly tapered cases were not suited to Smith and Wesson tools.

The Ideal Manufacturing Company produced a distinctive reloading tool which they designated the No. 2, especially for loading the Smith and Wesson line of target cartridges. It is described and pictured in the Ideal chapter.

IX

SCHUETZEN

It should be immediately acknowledged that the title of this chapter is misleading but, rather than have a long, involved one, it was chosen to represent a whole genre of specialized loading equipment used in single shot rifle target shooting.

The term "schuetzen" is a German word pertaining to "shooting." A "schuetzenfest" was a picnic where marksmanship was practiced. However, among American gun collectors and shooters it has been expanded to include firearms loosely patterned after or inspired by German target rifles.

German immigrants of the mid-nineteenth century brought with them an interest in target shooting at moderate distances using a distinctive target having narrow scoring rings. The shooting, conducted at a leisurely pace, was done with extremely heavy rifles from a standing position—what the great barrel maker Harry Pope referred to as "standing on your hind legs and shooting like a man." Peep sights, set triggers, and deep pronged buttplates were customary. At first these were percussion arms as seen, for example, in the fine pieces made by Milwaukee gunsmith John Munier. As soon as accurate reloadable cartridges came on the scene, single shot breech loaders began to be used for this purpose. Winchester, Ballard, Remington, Sharps, and others were produced in the "schuetzen" style. This coincided with the decline of long range Creedmoor-style shooting which required a 1000-yard range, target crews, and ten-pound rifles with their 100 grain charges that pummeled the shooter. With more pleasant shooting, mild loads in heavy rifles, and the need for only a 200-yard range "schuetzen-style" shooting appealed to the American target shooting fraternity.

In the pursuit of outstanding accuracy these rifles began to be fired from bench rests—not just to work up a load and/or to adjust sights, but as a contest in its own right. Accuracy was measured by the size of the group made by a string of shots rather than a point score. The standing or offhand position continued to have many adherents—often the bench rest shooters themselves. It was the quest for great accuracy which led to an array of specialized reloading implements, many made by the prominent barrel makers of the time, that are the subject of this chapter.

False muzzles to assure the bullet a concentric start down the barrel had been in use with muzzle loading rifles and that idea was carried over to custom barreled breach loaders. In the latter, the bullet was pushed down the barrel to a point just ahead of the chamber and the false muzzle removed. Then the primed and charged shell, a cardboard wad holding the powder in place, was inserted into the chamber for firing.

Prominent custom barrel makers like Harry Pope, A. O. Zischang, and others used this system. When smokeless powders became available in canisters for handloading, it was discovered that a small quantity of it followed by the balance of the charge of regular black powder made for comparable accuracy with but little residue left in the case or bore after firing. This became known as "duplex" loading. Powder measures were developed to throw such charges conveniently. One of these du-

A

plex measures, unmarked but attributed to the great Denver barrel maker, George C. Schoyen, is shown in (A). The small handle is moved to the right to release the priming charge and returned to drop the main charge. Opposite the measuring unit is a space for a re-decapper and a supply of bullets, primers, one or more shells (sometimes only one was used all day for uniformity), and even a breech seater. It was all contained in a neat oak box. When closed, the brass carrying handle on top holds the halves together to go to the range.

Harry M. Pope, the most famous barrel maker of that era, designed and produced the duplex measure shown in (B). Seen

B

C

in (C) is a Milwaukee Duplex Measure with windows to show the amount of powder remaining. Such long drop tubes were supposed to produce a more compact powder charge. San Francisco gunsmith Otto A. Bremer made a duplex measure of his own design which is shown in the California chapter, and the Ideal Manufacturing Company redesigned their No. 5 powder measure with an extra hopper to hold smokeless powder for duplex loading. They designated it their No. 6. It is shown in the chapter on Ideal products.

It was found that excellent accuracy could be obtained by loading the bullet directly into the rifling from the breech when

D

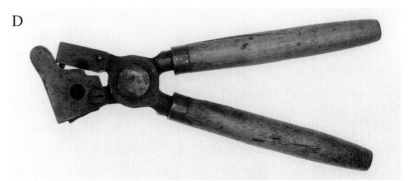

using duplex, and later straight smokeless loads. The grooved bullets were approximately bore diameter except the rear band which was larger to assure a good gas seal. Sometimes the band diameters were graduated to produce a sort of tapered bullet. They could be inserted with home-made seaters, but Ideal made them commercially in two types as described in that chapter. Since these bullets could not be sized by forcing them through a die but

E

had to be fired as cast, the cavity had to be precision work. A plain Pope mold, differing little from the standard Ideal mold is shown in (D). It was discovered that the bullet's base was its critical surface, a fact well established by the experimenter, Dr. Franklin Mann. Accordingly, Pope and others produced molds that poured from the nose and featured a "double cutoff" as shown in (E). Like Maynard molds they often had a lubricating hole at the hinge, sometimes indicated by the word "wax." A partially completed mold found in Pope's shop after his death is shown in (F). He went on to create a Universal bullet mold of which less than 100 were made. It had interchangeable blocks and could be adjusted to accommodate blocks of varying depth despite its double cutoff. The sprue was sheared off when the handles were opened. See (G).

F

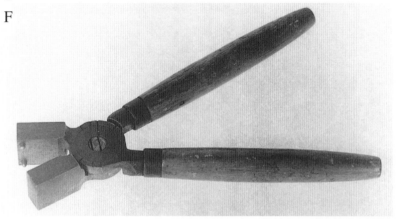

G

H

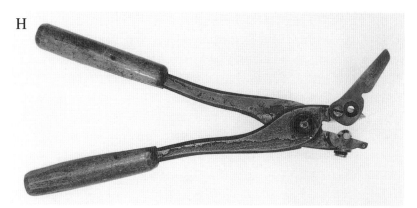

Other custom barrel makers had their own mold designs. A. O. Zischang made both (H) and (I). His shop was in Syracuse, New York. In (J) we see one by George Schoyen of Denver, Colorado.

I

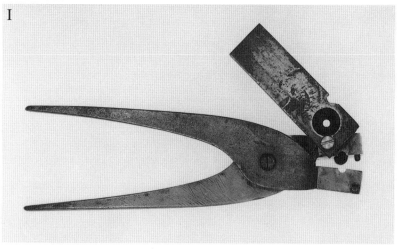

J

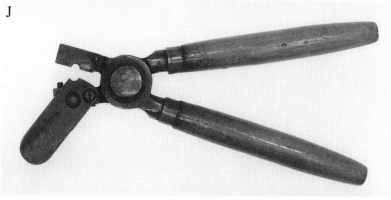

A Maynard bullet lubricator is shown in the Maynard chapter. Pope's version is shown in (K). The small handle fastens it to a bench while the larger one is turned to press the lubricant into the grooves of the bullet which is held in a receptacle on the end.

K

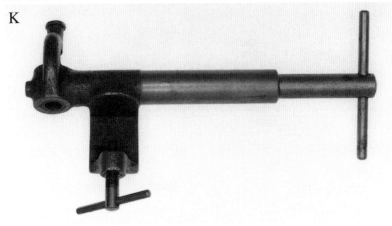

L

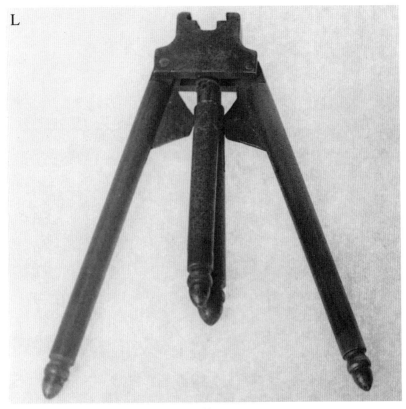

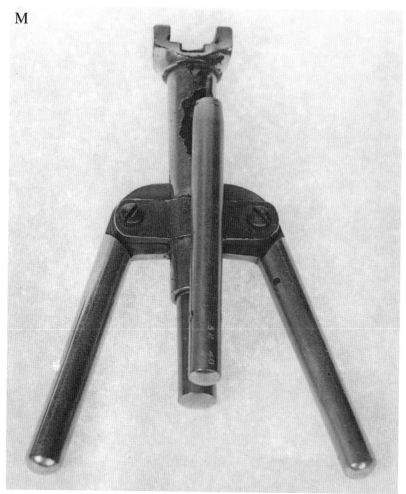

Removing the fired primer and replacing it was done with a variety of tools. Not requiring the precision of molds and lubricators nor the mechanisms of powder measures, they could be made by any gunsmith, machinist, or even ordinary shooters. Tools for this purpose are shown elsewhere but two prominent barrel makers are represented by Axel Peterson (L) and Pope (M). Both tools allow the reloader to feel the primer being seated. The user can adjust his hand pressure to assure full seating without crushing the primer and can instantly detect a misaligned primer—all very important for the uniformity of ignition required in highly accurate shooting. The Pope tool is marked with the "J. Stevens Arms & Tool Co." stamp indicating its manufacture during the short period Pope was employed by Stevens to supervise the making of his barrels and accessories. It also bears the 1902 patent date and, on the decapping rod, the caliber. Those of Pope's own manufacture are usually unmarked.

For more information on this era and style of shooting, the reader is directed to Ray M. Smith's *The Story of Pope's Barrels* and the various books by Gerald Kelver.

X

CALIFORNIA TOOLS AND MOLDS

The admonishment "to go west" and the "cries of gold in California" were but two of the reasons for the influx of settlers into California from the 1840's onward. Among those who trekked westward were gunsmiths and other entrepreneurs who would establish businesses catering to hunters, target shooters, and sportsmen. Some of the following were target shooters as well as businessmen. They would make and/or sell the reloading implements which we will detail here.

Otto A. Bremer, a San Francisco Gunsmith, made the canister style, nickel plated brass duplex powder measure shown in (A). It is marked "O.A.B.L CO SF" (Otto A. Bremer and Lewis Company, San Francisco) on the lid. The measure dropped the first charge which primed the case then dispensed the main charge.

Bremer also made brass, hand held, plier type re/decappers some of which were nickel plated. The one shown in (B) is marked "O.A.Bremer Maker San Francisco." A similar one is known stamped "STARS" and "233." With the Bremer re/decapper is shown a similar but not identical tool by J. Gruhler of Sacramento. These tools were frequently used by the Schuetzen target shooters who only needed to re/decap their cartridges, often while shooting at the range.

A

Bremer bullet molds have been reported but none have been observed by the authors; though swaged bullets bearing his name on the package have been seen.

In addition to his work as a gunsmith in San Francisco, Charles Douglas (C. D.) Ladd was a regular participant in the rifle matches of the 1870's. He produced a loading tool that is

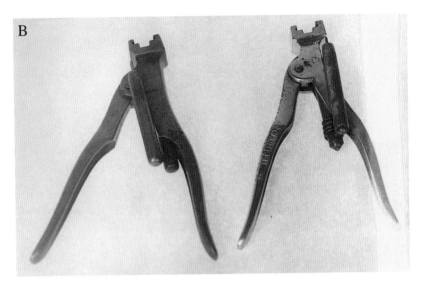

B

very similar to the Model 1882 Winchester tong tool. His tools have been found marked for calibers ranging from the .38-55 Ballard to the .45-70 Marlin. The one shown in (C) is marked "38/55 BAL C.D.LADD S.F." These rough cast tools use a push out pin to expel the cartridge from the seating/crimping chamber. Some are found still wearing vestiges of their original gold painted finish.

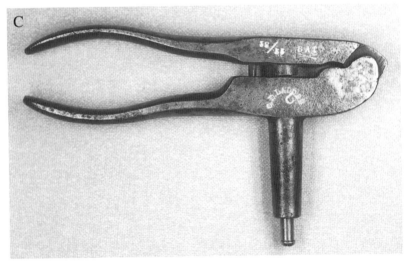

C

An extremely rare Ladd marked bullet mold is shown in (D). An equally rare box is shown in (E). This mold is marked

D

E

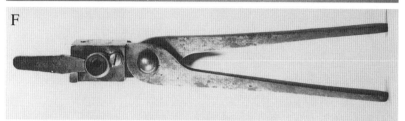

F

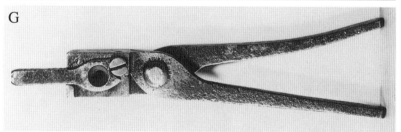

G

"C.D.Ladd S.F." Most Ladd and Ladd-type molds are found unmarked; many have been gold painted. However, the unmarked mold shown in (F) is the kind actually pictured on the box.

A Ladd and Smith marked mold is shown in (G). Its markings surround the hinge pin. This mold is substantially the same as the Ladd mold shown in (D). No Ladd and Smith marked reloading tools are known to the authors.

The following group of tools have been tentatively identified, although unmarked, as Ladd or "Ladd type" tools. They are rough cast, often gold painted, generally employing a push

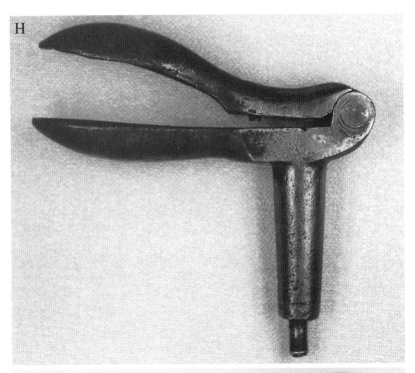

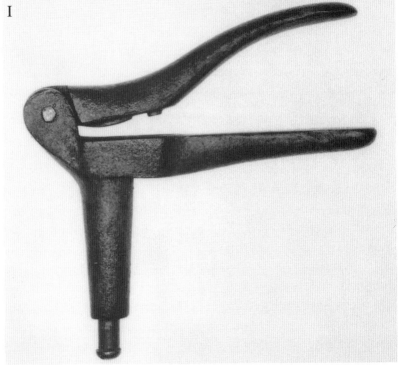

J

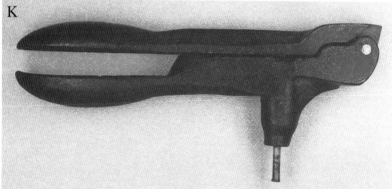

K

out pin to expel the loaded cartridge. The tool illustrated in (H) is a spoon handled tool with the end of its push out pin visible in the photograph. The tool in (I) is similar but with a slimmer style of handles.

A Ladd type tool with a detachable Berdan arm is shown in (J).

A rough cast, black painted Ladd type tool that is dimensionally very similar to the smaller sized Model 1875 Winchester tool is shown in (K). This tool also uses a push out pin to expel the completed cartridge.

A rough cast, gold painted capper is shown in (L). The round handle is squared off. It may have had a decapping pin like that on the Ballard tool, but in this case is most likely a wad seater. One that has a decapping pin similar to that on the Ballard tool accompanied a Peabody Martini rifle. A kindred unmarked

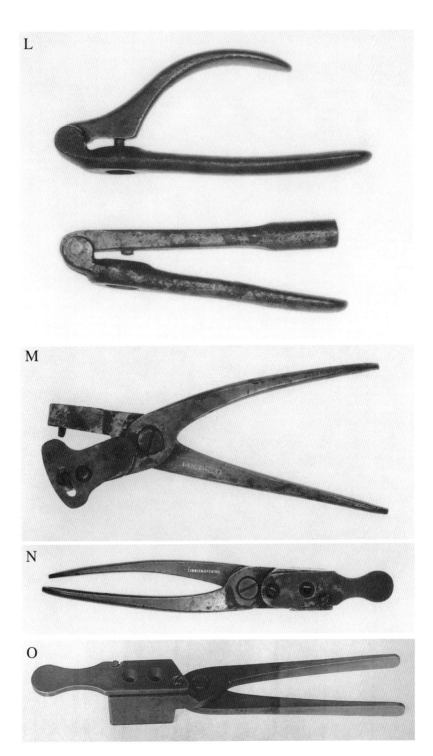

gold painted "hump back" capper is shown above it. Assigning these tools to Ladd is only an educated guess. C. D. Ladd tools were the subject of a July 1996 article in *The Gun Report*.

By 1875 Robert Liddle and Charles Kaeding's "Sportsmen's Emporium" was the largest firearms firm in San Francisco. With one known exception, all of the Liddle and Kaeding bullet molds encountered are single-cavity brass molds with an iron sprue plate and pivot screw. Most are stamped "Liddle & Kaeding" on both the top and bottom handles. The mold shown in (M) has a "Remington style" sprue plate very similar to the ones found on the later style Remington bullet molds. What appears to be a capper is the alignment pin. The mold pictured in (N) has the more commonly encountered sprue plate. The tool in (O) illustrates a rare two cavity Liddle and Kaeding mold. Liddle and Kaeding bullet molds are the subject of a November 1997 article in *The Gun Report*.

XI

IDEAL

From the 1880's until well into the twentieth century the field of handloading was dominated by the Ideal Manufacturing Company. Today's collectors are constantly reminded of its products as they encounter their familiar nickel plated tong tools. Among the reasons for this dominance would have to be that they were good products that worked well; they came in a variety of models to suit any shooter's needs including shotshell implements; and they were the sole product of the company, not a sideline as with Winchester, Remington, Smith and Wesson, Whitney, and almost every other producer of reloading implements. Another factor was the company's willingness to accept special orders. A look through the earlier Ideal Handbooks shows a huge selection of bullets available. Many bullet molds began as special orders from individuals which were then listed in the handbooks often with the designer's name identifying them. A modest charge was made to cover the cost of a new "cherry" for cutting the cavity which was then stored away ready for future orders. The less frequently ordered molds were put on the "Special List" at a small increase in price.

An important factor in Ideal's success was the *Ideal Handbook* which would go through many editions serving both as a catalog and instruction manual. According to Phil Wahl, its publication began in 1891 although Ideal products had been on the market for several years by then—probably since 1885. Reloading implements were illustrated from the first edition of the Ideal Handbook onward. A chart listing the early Ideal Handbooks is shown in (A).

The principal Ideal Co. product was a line of tong type tools based on John Barlow's patents of March 11 and December 23, 1884. Although the tools are marked February 11 and December 23, 1884, the first patent was actually issued on March 11, 1884. (See patents in the Appendix.) An excellent compact reference to them is *Field Guide to Identifying the Ideal Tong*

A CHRONOLOGY OF IDEAL HANDBOOKS

Handbook No.	Year(s) Published	Handbook No.	Year(s) Published
1st Ed.	1891	20	1910 *
2nd Ed.	1891	21	1910 *
3	1892	22	1911 *
4	1893	23	1912 *
5	1894	24	1913 *
6	1895	25	1914 *
7	1896	26	1915, 16 *
8	1896	27	1926
9	1897	28	1927, 28, 29
10	1898	29	1930
11	1899	30	1931, 32, 33
12	1900	31	1934, 35
13	1901	32	1936, 37, 38
14	1902	33	1939
15	1903	34	1940 – 1947
16	1904	35	1948
17	1906	36	1949
18	1907	37	1950
19	1908	38	1951
		39	1953
Lyman Centennial Journal 1878 – 1978	1978		

* Years that the Marlin firearms Co. owned the Ideal Mfg. Co.

Tools by George McCluney.

Ideal assigned a model number to each tool in their line. They will be discussed in numerical order after which the company's miscellaneous products will be delineated.

First for consideration is the No. 1 tong loading tool. Like all the others, it is of nickel plated steel and bears the company identification and patent dates as well as its caliber. It is this model that introduced the Ideal line and is shown in the 1885 Marlin catalog. With the introduction of the 1888 Marlin catalog the line had increased to several tools. The No. 1 tool has a bullet mold on the end and was made to reload pistol and small rifle cartridges of the period. It is distinguished from other Ideal models by the absence of a bullet sizer. The seating/crimping chamber is not adjustable. The capping feature can be found in the handle or on the early specimens on the mold end. There is a significantly smaller and very scarce version of this tool. A typical No. 1 tool with its box is shown in (B). According to Phil Wahl, this model continued in production until 1926.

Introduced in the earliest listings was the No. 2 tool specifically designed for the Smith and Wesson .32-44, .38-44, re-

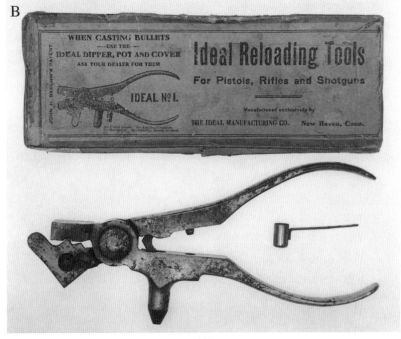

volving rifle, regular .38 S & W revolver cartridges and, rarely, .44 Russian target cartridges. The first two of these were brought out along with the Smith and Wesson Number 3 New Model revolver. The second figure in these cartridge designations can be misleading. It does not refer to the powder charge but to the pistol's frame size. Also this .38-44 should not be confused with a similarly named, but much later cartridge which was actually a heavily loaded .38 Special to be used in the .44 size frame. The bullet seating chamber has an adjustable plunger to regulate seating depth. The single cavity mold may be "cherried" to cast either a conventional bullet or a round ball for the sport of "gallery" shooting which was then popular. Some have the capper in the handle while others have it on the mold end. This model was dropped in 1909 at the same time Smith and Wesson discontinued the New Model Number 3 revolvers. Due to their very specialized purpose, these No. 2 tools are a relatively scarce item. The one illustrated in (C) is for the .38-44 caliber.

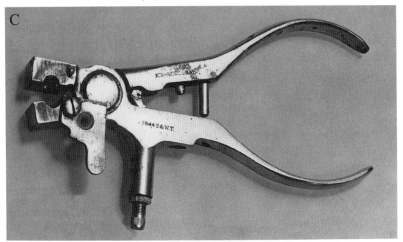

Called by Ideal "the Rifle Crank's very own," the No. 3 tool was designed for great versatility though like all other Ideal loading tools it had to be ordered for one specific cartridge. There was no attached mold. It was available with either a single or a double adjustable chamber. A muzzle (case mouth) resizer interchangeable with the chamber was also offered. It was made in the full range of centerfire rifle cartridges from the .22 Extra Long

Maynard to the .50 cal. Sharps. Three sizes of tools were needed to cover this range of calibers. It was dropped soon after World War II. A tool with a double-adjustable chamber, decapping pin, and powder dipper is shown in (D).

D

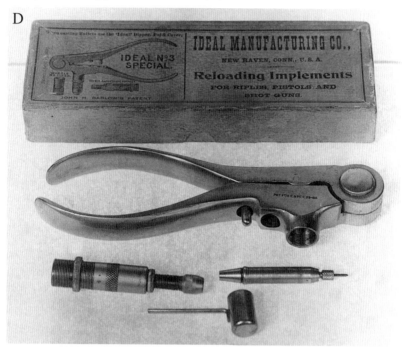

The No. 4 tool came in two variants. Its basic type was like the No. 1 but with the addition of a bullet sizing feature in the lower handle. See (E). The rare No. 4 Special, available for only a few years, differed only in having an adjustable chamber.

E

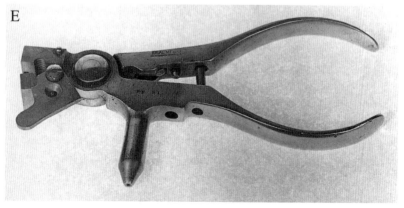

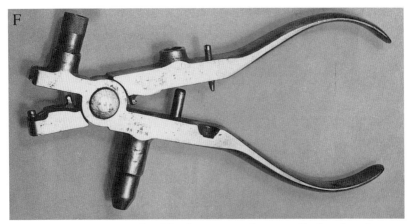

Now comes the Ideal tong tool most distinctive in appearance. It was designated the No. 5 but was also given the name "The Armory Tool." One of these scarce tools is shown in (F). It was designed specifically for reloading the U.S. Government .45-70 cartridge and grew out of the extensive reloading of this caliber by National Guard units and similar groups doing military style shooting. It is very rarely seen in any other caliber though specimens are known for Colt, Bullard, Marlin, Maynard, and Winchester cartridges attesting once again to Ideal's willingness to oblige any customer's request. The No. 5 differs from other Ideal tools in three respects. Immediately apparent is the case mouth resizer jutting up ahead of the hinge with the capper adjacent to it. Also noteworthy is the bullet sizing plunger that pushes the bullet upward instead of down. Catalogs illustrate it without a Berdan decapping feature but at least some, like (F), had the semi-circular cutout and chisel for removing them. Available at additional cost was a double adjustable seating/crimping chamber that would interchange with the case mouth (muzzle) sizer to accommodate the government 500 grain bullet. Since its seating depth could be controlled, it could also seat any other length of bullet. For loading round balls for the popular sport of indoor "gallery" shooting a special chamber was available. Otherwise the reloader was limited to the plain fixed chamber. Although made from Ideal's earliest years until 1906, not many of these were sold and they are quite scarce.

G

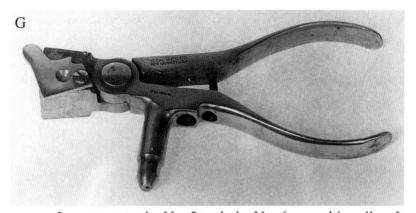

In contrast to the No. 5 tool, the No. 6 was a big seller. It was a larger version of the popular No. 4 tool with an integral mold, fixed chamber, and sizer in the handle. While the former loaded pistol and small rifle cartridges, the No. 6 handled the larger rifle cartridges from .32-35 Stevens and Maynard up to the .50-95 and .50-100-450 Winchester. A basic No. 6 tool is shown in (G). To accommodate this range of calibers, it was made in two distinct sizes. In addition, there was a special No. 6-A tool made for and sold by Stevens which is discussed in that chapter. The plain, non-adjustable seating chamber was standard but either single or double adjustable chambers were available at extra cost. In the early 1930's some of these tools were marketed for pistol size cartridges having removable mold blocks of the type seen on all the later Ideal (Lyman) molds up to the present time. Despite their large size they were listed as No. 4 tools in catalogs. One of these is shown in (H).

H

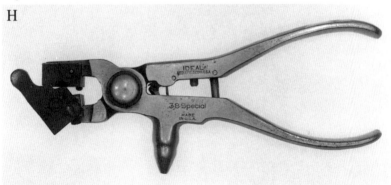

The next tool is a "mirror image" of the No. 6 tool described above. This variant has been dubbed the "left handed model." It has been found in both frame sizes and in Colt, Marlin, Sharps, Stevens, and Winchester calibers ranging from .32-40 through .45-90. The tool pictured in (I) is marked .40-70 S.S. This tool is considered scarce.

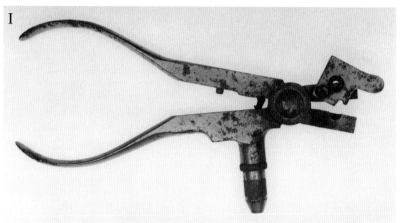

I

The No. 7 tool is almost certainly the rarest of the Ideal tong tools. They were offered for only a few years in the late 1800's. It is marked "44 CAL. X L SHOT C'T'G." Since it was designed for a shot cartridge only, it has no provision for bullet sizing. The chamber is non-adjustable. It was designed to load a special long-cased version of the .44 WCF cartridge which was recommended by Ideal for pest control and taxidermy specimens in firearms of that caliber. Another use may have been by the "Wild West" shows of the time. Performers fired shot through smooth bored rifles and sometimes pistols at glass balls thrown into the air. Shot was used for the safety of the public but had the bonus of making hitting the target easier than with a bullet. The firm of Merwin and Hulbert of New York City was listed as the source of these special cartridge cases. The case was longer than the usual .44 WCF with the forward part in the shape of the regular bullet. This configuration would have allowed them to function in a magazine rifle far better than the usual hollow wood or paper shell used in shot loads. These cartridges are quite similar to the "5 in 1" movie blanks; but, of course, designed only for this one caliber. A few shotguns were made to fire this relatively unknown cartridge and one tool was reported with a boxed Marble "Game Getter" firearm. Until further information surfaces on the rare and elusive No. 7 tool, little else can be offered the reader. One is shown in (J).

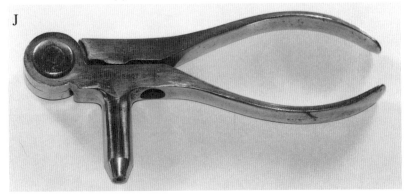

J

Many of the early cartridges, both rim and centerfire, were made with a bullet of the same diameter as the *outside* of the shell. Most .22 rimfires are of this type. In them the base of the bullet had a reduced diameter known as a "heel" which fit the *inside* diameter of the case mouth. The problem, as mentioned earlier, was that the sticky lubricant was applied to that portion of the bullet extending outside the case, not inside on grooves designed to hold it. Consequently it rubbed off or else picked up dirt and lint while being carried and handled. Then a way was devised to utilize a bullet that would seat in the case with the mouth covering the lubricated grooves and would still fill the bore upon firing. This was done by copying the famed Minié ball of Civil War fame. The undersized bullet expanded to full size when the powder charge exploded causing the bullet's "skirt" surrounding the deep hollow base to press outward into the rifling. The cartridges loaded by the No. 8 tool utilized this principal. A No. 8 tool is shown in (K). These cartridges would interchange with the heeled version since both were of the same diameter but the hollow base bullet sat deeper in the case with only its curve or ogive showing. These newer cases were ordinarily made a bit longer to accommodate the regular powder charge plus the additional covered portion of the bullet.

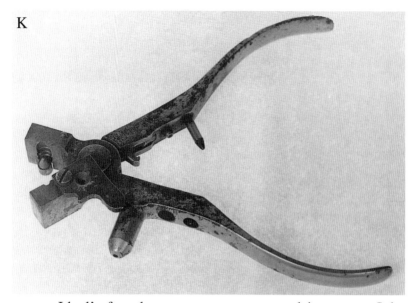

K

Ideal's founder, owner, manager, and inventor—John Barlow—patented on February 10, 1891 a system for casting the hollow base bullets used in this tool. Instead of pouring the molten lead into the base end of the cavity, it was poured into the nose end while a plug produced the hollow base. When the mold was opened the plug, still attached, moved sideways sufficiently to release the bullet. It can be better understood by examining the patent in the Appendix. At first these tools were made only for reloading the .38 Long cartridge used in the then new Colt military revolver. Later several more calibers were offered from .32 L I L to .455 British. The letters L I L stand for "Long Inside Lubricated." Other models and other makes are found with an "O" instead of an "I" to indicate outside lubricated, the earlier type but still in extensive use. In addition to the nose pour bullet mold, this tool is recognizable by the pointed end on the bullet sizing plunger which fits into the hollow base bullet keeping it aligned in the sizing die.

Following in sequence would be the No. 9 tool. But where is it? It does not seem to exist; at least none have been reported. Perhaps it was an experimental model that never reached production. At least for the time being it must remain a frustrating gap in the Ideal line.

This brings us to No. 10. It is identical to the No. 3 tool except for the presence of a "priming hook." Rimless cartridges were coming into vogue in the very late 1800's because of their superior functioning in modern smokeless magazine military rifles. Due to their rim design, these cartridges would slip through the capping receptacle of a No. 3 tool. The No. 10 was designed to solve this problem. It had an adjustable chamber with the addition of a "priming hook" which engaged the groove in the shell's head holding the case while the primer was pressed into place. An improvement on the detachable hook was a sliding catch which was permanently affixed to the tool and thus was not easily lost. The No. 10 tool appeared in 1900 initially for the new 6mm Lee Navy cartridge and the 7mm Mauser with the promise that as other rimless cartridges came along Ideal would make tools for them. By the time Ideal Handbook Number 30 was published, the list had expanded to 34 different calibers. This tool was developed just in time to load the new .30-'03 and '06 cartridges. While not rare, the No. 10 tools are not common either. A No. 10 tool is shown in (L).

Immediately after World War II the company, by that time owned by the Lyman Gunsight Corp., reorganized and simpli-

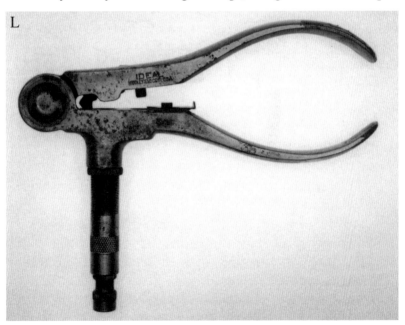

L

fied its offerings resulting in an all-purpose tool designed to re-place all others. By combining the No. 3 and the No. 10 they came up with the Model 310. Gone were the tools with integral molds and all the variations great and small that delight and some-times puzzle today's collectors. A simplified identification chart is shown in (M).

M

IDEAL LOADING TOOL
IDENTIFICATION CHART

NUMBER	DISTINGUISHING FEATURES	MOLD
One	non-adjustable; no bullet sizer	Yes
Two	for S & W target cartridges; adjustable seater, no crimper	Yes
Three	singe or double adjustable chamber	No
Four	smaller cartridges; bullet sizer	Yes
Five	case mouth sizer and capper on end	No
Six	for large cartridges, sizer	Yes
Seven	.44 X.L. shot only, no sizer	No
Eight	hollow base bullet; pointed plunger	Yes
Ten	"priming hook" or plate	No

Now we go on to the Ideal bullet molds, powder measures, and other paraphernalia in their extensive line. It should be noted that from 1884 through 1893 Ideal products were distributed by Marlin, Colt, Stevens, Maynard, Bullard, J. P. Moore and Sons, and J. P. Lovell Arms as well as by themselves.

The very first Ideal molds were, of course, those integral with their tools as on the No. 1; but by the time the first Ideal Handbook came out, separate molds were listed. At first the caliber and company name were stamped on the cutoff plate. Early ones had pinned handles; later ones ferrules. Their basic design was to continue until about 1930 when molds with detachable blocks appeared and were listed as the "Improved Ideal Single Mould." The company pointed out that this mold would gradually supersede the previous one. This "improved" type is the one familiar to today's shooters. Ideal molds were available for regular bullets plus round balls, "express" (meaning hollow point), and blanks "ready to cut." For "lovers of fine tools" there was an extra heavy, finely finished mold featuring polished cocobolo handles at a premium price. With the increasing variety of special bullet designs came the practice of assigning a distinguishing number to each in which the first three digits reflected the diameter of the bullet in thousandths of an inch and the remaining one(s) the specific bullet design. Except for the No. 1 loading tool, all Ideal molds cast bullets slightly oversize to allow for sizing. An example of the basic Ideal mold with pinned handles is shown in (N).

There was interest among the shooting fraternity in an adjustable mold that would permit the reloader to vary the bullet weight by altering the bullet's length. The Ideal Company's solution is seen in two separate models: one for grooved bullets

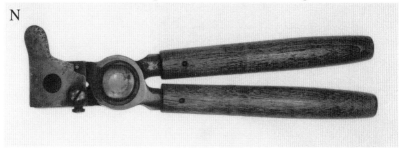

N

and the other for smooth paper patched ones. They are extensively discussed in the January 1993 issue of *The Gun Report.* The grooved model, termed the "Perfection," was based on a February 10, 1891 patent. A plug was screwed in and out of the mold to set the bullet's length and the lead poured from the nose end. See (O). They are found from .22 to .45 caliber. Apparently a few were made for casting paper-patched bullets.

The usual paper-patched model was called the "Cylindrical Adjustable Mould" and could be had in calibers ranging from .25 to .45. It was based upon a January 10, 1893 patent. In it lead is poured from the base end, the sprue sheared, and a plunger pushed up to eject the bullet. One is seen in (P). It worked so well that the No. 5 Handbook states that they would no longer make them using the hinged design.

O

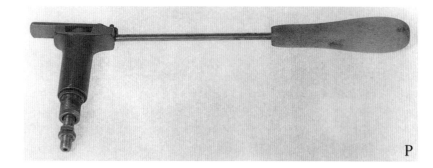

P

The mold shown in (Q) is, in one sense, adjustable. It is marked "38-330 Rabbeth" and makes a heavy paper-patched bullet for target shooting with the .38-55 cartridge. Francis J. Rabbeth was a prominent shooter on the famous Walnut Hill range and wrote under the pen name "J. Francis." This bullet uses an unusual once-around rectangular patch applied just before firing and seated directly into the rifling with a special breech seater. Bullet length is determined by a plug at its base and it was poured from the nose. Another of these molds has been reported accompanied by an assortment of plugs for different bullet weights.

Indoor, short range "gallery" shooting was popular in the 19th century. Usually the bullet was a round ball seated deeply

Q

in the case against a small charge of powder. These loads were very popular in Smith and Wesson's target revolvers but were used in all calibers through the .45-70. An improvement was the "collar button" bullet. It had the advantages of having two good bearing surfaces to keep the bullet aligned and a generous grease groove whereas a round ball had one bore contact with the lubricant smeared on its upper surface. Collar button bullets weighed the same as the equivalent sized round ball. See (R).

Another Ideal development that enjoyed some success was the casting of a separate tip for the bullet. A November 1993 article in *The Gun Report* explored this interesting variation. The idea was that the tip would be cast of a softer, or rarely, harder alloy than the rest of the bullet providing a soft or hard point. It is probable that the first of these was designed for the familiar .45-70 but there were several others down to the .22 Savage. The tip, cast separately and allowed to cool, was put into the regular cavity and the lead poured in. A mushroom shaped shank on the tip held it in place. Although the tip and bullet required separate molds, one was reported in which both cavities were "cherried" in the same mold. One is shown in (S).

For reloading in quantity Ideal had a massive bench press and an armory mold. The mold weighing about four pounds and

R

S

T

casting six bullets at a time is shown in (T). Thus we leave the subject of Ideal bullet molds and look at some powder measures.

The first Ideal powder measures were the dippers supplied with each tool. Before the century's end, the "Universal Powder Measure" would enter the Ideal line. One of these scarce items, its hopper missing, is shown in (U). Its graduations are in both grains and drams and the charge is regulated by two slides, one working within the other. This idea was to be a continuing feature of Ideal measures. When other powder measures were developed by Ideal, this one was designated No. 1.

The No. 2 was similar but with a small extra hopper to hold smokeless (or a different granulation of black) powder for loading "duplex" style loads. Nos. 3 and 4 were shotshell chargers and are thus outside the purview of this study.

U

No. 5 replaced the No. 1 and was produced over many decades until it was superseded by the modern No. 55. It differs from the No. 1 primarily in that its large rectangular hopper is integral with the rest of the measure. It also has an attached knocker to jar loose powder grains hung up inside the measure. Like the No. 1 it has a double slide adjustment. A variant had a single slide with convenient "micrometer" adjustment but the company indicated that it was not well suited to dispensing pistol charges. A No. 5 powder measure is shown in (V).

V

The No. 6 measure was designed specifically for duplex loading. It has a smaller smokeless powder hopper adjoining the main black powder one. Each has its own adjustment. Otherwise it is like the No. 5. See (W).

The final powder measure to be considered is the odd "Ideal Loading Flask." It was patented on June 11, 1889 by the F. J. Rabbeth mentioned above and preceded the numbered mea-

W

sures. It was touted as "the only flask in the world that can measure powder accurately for rifles, pistols, and shotguns or that has a range from 3 up to 135 grains and from 1/4 up to 5 drachms." It is constructed of nickel plated brass with a capacity of 3/4 pound of black powder. Shotgun smokeless powder could also be dispensed following a table of equivalents supplied by the company. Its operation is better understood by actually handling one. Briefly, it is held with the measuring chamber downward, filling the preset chamber, and the cut-off plate returned to its "neutral" position. Then, with the flask reversed, the charge is released to drop through a diagonal tube within the flask and out into the shell. A "rattler" is located on the discharge end to free any powder caught in the tube. One of these novel flasks is shown in (X). They have been called "Creedmoor" flasks though this style of shooting was largely passé by the time of its appearance. They are quite scarce, a situation aggravated by the fact that they are sought by both flask and loading tool collectors.

The late 19th and early 20th century was a period when much attention was given to achieving the ultimate in accuracy. Creedmoor target shooting—with its punishing heavily loaded cartridges fired in rifles which were not permitted to exceed 10 pounds and needing 1000-yard ranges—gave way to shorter distances and milder loads of the Schuetzen-style shooting introduced by German immigrants. There were a number of fine single shot rifles on the market including Ballard, Stevens, Remington-Hepburn, and Winchester as well as others made by first-class custom makers. The Ideal Manufacturing Company was devoted exclusively to serving the shooter. The company developed a variety of tools to perform specific operations requested by the shooting fraternity.

Many shooters, desiring to reduce the bullet distortion caused by its short jump from the case neck into the barrel's rifling, elected to seat the bullet directly into the rifling followed by the case loaded with powder held by a card wad. Thus came about the bullet or ball seater sometimes called a breech seater to distinguish it from a similarly named but different tool. Certainly the earliest ones were hand made using fired cases. The Ideal Company's response is shown with its box in (Y) which could be adjusted to vary the distance that the bullet was seated into the bore. Later a simpler one came out which while still functional was less expensive. It was designated the No. 1 and the adjustable model the No. 2.

In this kind of shooting the bullet was not seated in the case much less crimped so Ideal came out with a tool which only re and decapped. It had a removable decapping pin and case holder so the same basic tool could be used for different calibers, a convenience for both the shooter and the company. Some of

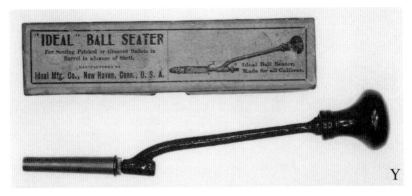

Y

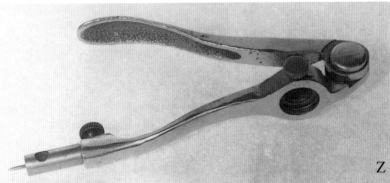

Z

these tools have the shell holder completely encircled by metal while others have a part circle holder itself only partly enclosed. See (Z). Some shooters, in their quest for ultimate accuracy, used the same case for all their shooting until the primer pocket became enlarged and the case discarded. This tool was convenient for such a practice. Its primary drawback was that a very strong push was required to expel the fired primer. Ideal's answer to the problem was the tool seen with its box in (AA). It had the leverage necessary for easier decapping and for seating the new primer and could even be bench mounted yet was as compact as the previous model. It became the No. 2 while the other was designated the No. 1.

AA

Ideal tong tools, except the No. 1, were provided with a bullet sizing die; but if the shooter wanted to size his bullets separately or preferred a slightly different diameter, he could purchase Ideal's bullet-sizing tool. The interchangeable dies were marked with the caliber. Besides the convenience in handling, the die pivoted in the tool body assuring concentric alignment of bullet, plunger, and die. One of these tools is shown in (BB).

When loading regular charges of black powder, the case was filled to capacity except for the space taken up by the seated portion of the bullet. Thus there was never a problem with bullets slipping back into the case, even in tubular magazines. Dense smokeless powders, however, taking up less space, did not fill the case and support the bullet so that even crimped bullets might slip back into the case. The solution provided by Ideal was its ingenious "Shell Indentor." The empty case was slipped onto a fluted mandrel and four equidistant dents were put in the neck of the case stopping the bullet from moving beyond that point. Mandrels were interchangeable to accommodate other calibers. Since a regular decapping pin could not enter an indented case, one with the same flutes as the mandrel was offered for use in tools as was one with a wood handle for pushing out the primer by hand. One is shown with its box in (CC).

Ideal produced an "Armory Loading Outfit" for quantity reloading and the "Lightning" decapper was a part of it. A smart rap on the curved top of the plunger drove the fired primer out and a spring returned it ready for the next shell. They were made only to deprime .30-40, .30-'06, and .38 Special cases, for these were the calibers most likely to be reloaded in quantity. One is shown with its box in (DD).

Occasionally Ideal tools will be found marked "Marlin" reflecting a time between 1910 when Marlin bought the company to about 1916. Molds of the Marlin period do not normally

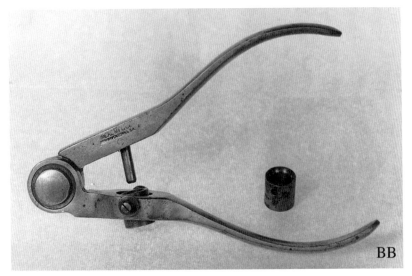

BB

bear the Marlin stamp though their boxes are so marked. Still later, in 1925, the Ideal Manufacturing Company was bought by the Lyman Gunsight Company and continues under that banner today.

CC

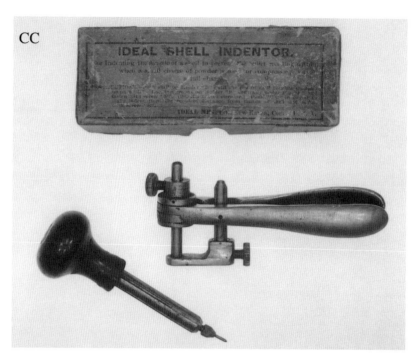

DD

XII

MISCELLANEOUS

Although the focus of this study is on implements for reloading fully self-contained breech loading metallic cartridges, an exception is made for the Burnside outfit shown in (A). Over 50,000 Burnside carbines were made for use in the Civil War period. Like the Sharps, Maynard, Gallager, Smith and others the ignition source came from an external percussion cap with the flash passing through the base of the cartridge. A sample Burnside cartridge is shown. The largest object in the photo is the body of the tool which held the case while the bullet was seated. Adjacent is the heavy top portion of the tool which seated the bullet in the case. On the far right are the parts of a case sizer or bullet swage. This is a rare outfit indeed.

The interesting combination tool and mold shown in (B) is a Lyon and Boyd (of Chadron, Nebraska) tool bearing the company name, patents of March 1, 1887 and February 21, 1888, plus the caliber. All markings appear on the top surface of the

A

B

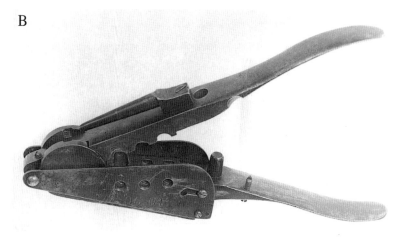

sprue plate. There are three cavities of which one is extra long for a heavy bullet and requiring a cutout on the bottom plate. On some specimens one cavity casts a round ball. Opening the handles shears off the sprues. Present are both the regular decapper and Berdan chisel. Bullet seating takes place inside one handle as in the 1881 Marlin tool. Its likely predecessor is (C). It has a filed-out and sanded appearance and bears only the stamping "J. W. Boyd." Like the one above, it has three cavities; in this case short, long, and roundball. All of the Lyon and Boyd and Boyd tools are quite scarce.

The compact little Kingsland re-decapper shown in (D) has its patent date of April 23, 1878 cast into one side and the outline of a rifle on the other. It is nickel plated iron. The spindle

C

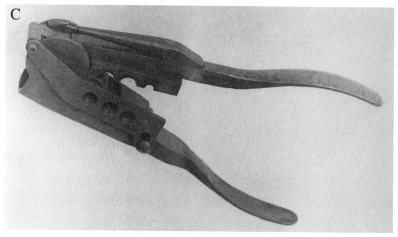

D

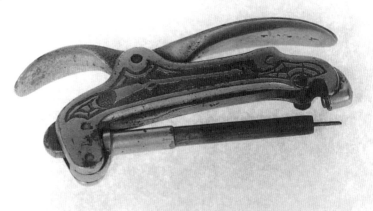

swings aside to accept the fired case. Pressing the short lever causes the decapping pin to move forcing out the fired primer. With the case still in place, pressing the longer lever withdraws the pin and seats the new primer. Another version has a more rounded body, is painted gold, and has its patent date on the side and caliber "40" on the spindle.

E

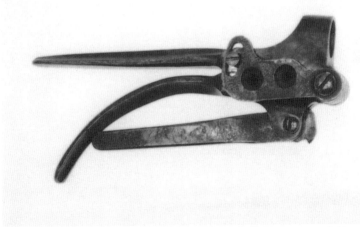

The Clews combination reloading tool and mold is shown in (E). It was the subject of an April 1988 article in *The Gun Report*. Its only marking is "Patent Oct. 3, 1871." This patent has to do with its Berdan decapping feature which, like so many, does not work particularly well. It is made of brass and casts two pistol size bullets of about .44 caliber. The steel arm has a decapping chisel which can be brought around to engage the primer when the case is in place and the oddly curved handle is open. This arm also seats the primer. Clews tools are very scarce.

F

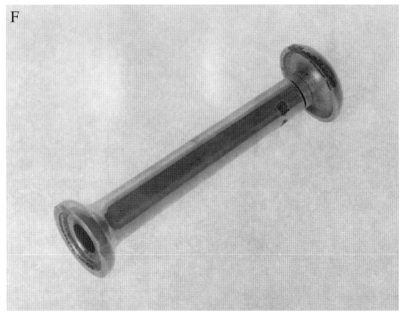

In (F) we see a ball seater very much like those supplied for Ballard rifles. There are no markings whatsoever. It is nicely polished and nickeled. Unlike the Ballard tool which has a notch in the base for prying out the completed cartridge, this one has a groove surrounding the bottom orifice so that a knife blade can pry it out. Normally there is very little friction between the cartridge and the ball seater making the task of prying out the loaded round relatively easy.

Really out of the realm of strictly hand loading tools but most interesting is the bench capper shown in (G). A product of the "guilded age" it has a gold paint finish. The base is made to be held in place by screws. It performs only the capping function and must have been used to speed up that process, perhaps at a small cartridge manufactory or armory. The holder is correct for the .45-70 cartridge. There are no markings, but its design suggests that it is not one of a kind though no others have been reported.

A truly rare tool is the Brown Variform reloader shown in (H). There is an excellent treatment on the subject of Bullard reloading tools by James Zupan in G. Scott Jamieson's *Bullard Arms*. This tool was featured in Bullard catalogs in the middle 1880's. But after a brief period, this tool gave way to a multipart "straight line" tool of Bullards' own design. One of these in 40-75 Bullard with its box is shown in (I).

Among the rarely encountered loading tools are those made by the Providence Tool Company of Providence, Rhode

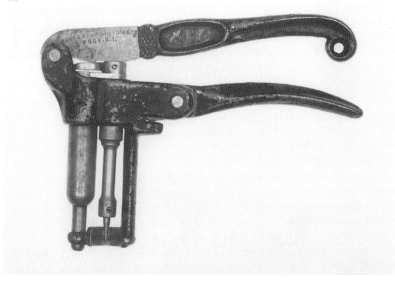

Island. This company manufactured a line of military and fine sporting rifles using the Peabody and Peabody-Martini actions. While their military arms are quite common, the sporting and target arms are scarce and sought after by collectors of single shot rifles. Despite the rather small number of arms made, the company designed its own line of cartridges. James Grant's *Single Shot Rifles* devotes a full chapter to this company and its products.

The tool shown in (J) is the capper. It is stamped "Man f d by Prov Tool Co." and "Prov. R. I." encircling the hinge. The caliber, "50" is stamped inconspicuously within the jaws. This tool, except the hinge area, has a black "Japanned" finish. There is a return spring to hold the jaws in the open position. The capping pin is of large diameter as befits one used to seat the broad Berdan primers of the time.

J

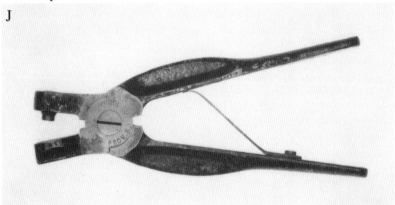

In (K) is seen the unusual decapping mate to the capper just described. However, unlike the capper, the only marking is its caliber ".45" on the hinge. The finish is the same. The fired case is placed in the cradle and the handles closed causing the chisel to pierce the primer. Then the cradle is pivoted upward prying the case away from its primer. The depth of the chisel cut is controlled by a set screw rather than by threads as usually seen on other tools.

There was an equally odd bullet seater of similar construction shown in the catalog. An early form of capper is shown on the cover of *American Single Shot Rifle News* for November-December 1995.

K

A. C. Gould's *Modern American Rifles*, first published in 1892, was the source of the identification of (L) which is a Harwood bullet lubricating pump. It is nickel plated and, like other pumps, forces the lubricant directly into the grooves of the bullet—a much cleaner, more efficient, and exacting way to lubricate.

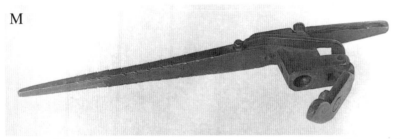

Shown in (M) is a rather crude but ingenious bullet mold which may never have been produced in quantity. It was in an old hunter's box, accompanied by a Ballard re-decapper, a C. D. Ladd-type mold, and a supply of the scarce .40-90 Ideal Everlasting Ballard nickel plated cases and loads. There are no markings. The long, pointed tang is designed to fit into a wooden handle to protect the caster's hands from heat. Its unusual feature is the base which is held closed under spring tension but which pops open when its arm is lightly struck. The plate has a convex bump to form the hollow base of the bullet in which to tuck the tail of the paper patch.

In (N) we see a still unidentified bullet mold marked with only the number "42" on the bottom. It is made of brass with a

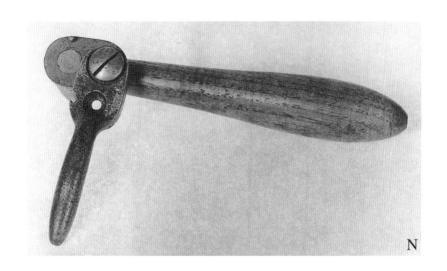

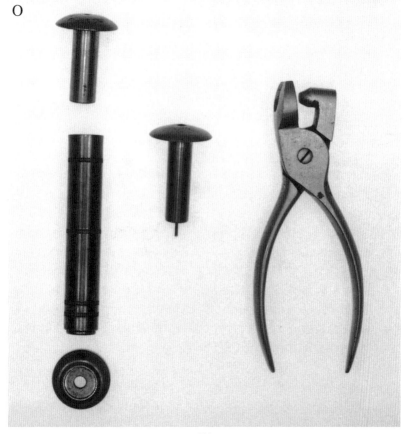

steel cutoff and a varnished wood handle. Its design brings to mind those made for the Civil War Starr revolvers, but this bullet is a full inch long and weighs over 300 grains. It could, of course, cast bullets for a muzzle loading "slug" gun, but Frank Wesson reportedly made centerfire cartridge rifles in this caliber. Another possibility is the .42 Russian Berdan cartridge.

This seems like an appropriate place to show a Frank Wesson loading outfit. See (O). It includes a three-piece ball seater (plunger, body, and base), decapper, and capper. The old style primers were thin and fairly soft, so a blow of the hand sufficed to drive them out.

P

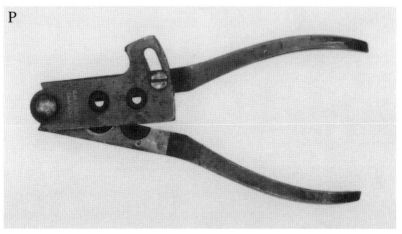

The next items are of Colt manufacture. Most collectors are familiar with the Colt molds for percussion arms. These are for their cartridge revolvers. The mold shown in (P) is readily identifiable as a Colt product looking virtually identical to those for their percussion arms. However, it dates from 1873 and casts bullets for the then new .45 caliber Colt Single Action Army revolver which, in recent years has come to be known erroneously as the .45 Long Colt. A close-up of the side of the mold (Q) reveals the earlier stamping for the ".36 R" bullet. Although this is a "navy" caliber, the "R" is for rifle and doubtless is a leftover mold for the revolving rifle. The former caliber has been canceled out and "45 A" substituted showing its new caliber.

In (R) we see a Colt bullet mold with a hook capper. This most primitive type of capper is similar to those seen in some

Q

B. G. I. Co. loading outfits. The hook engages the rim, pivoting on it to force the primer into place. The small protuberance seats the primer all the way down into the primer pocket and below the surface of the case head. It is shown "up-side-down" to better illustrate the hook. Colt is known to have made a very simple set of loading tools to accompany these molds but they are rare and, like so many multi-piece sets, go unrecognized, even as reloading items.

R

    The well-made but strange, double-jointed tool shown in (S) bears this stamping: "Z. C. TALBOT PAT. AP'LD FOR 32." Like so many other early tools, it performs only the functions of removing and replacing primers.

    Still another such tool is shown in (T); but, in this case it

S

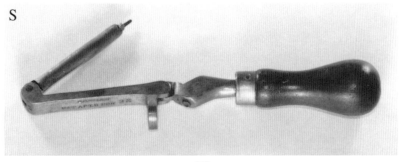

T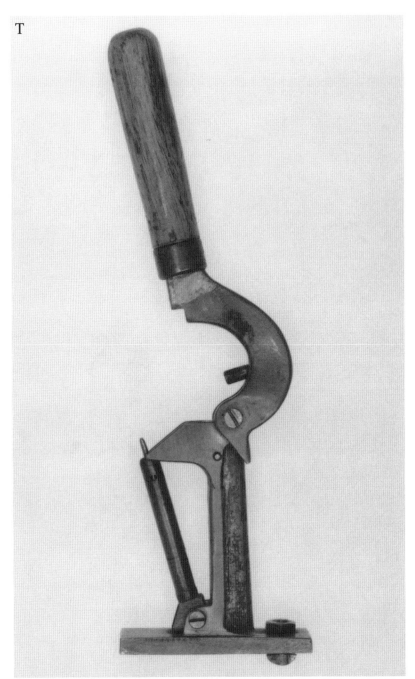

is designed to mount on a bench. William F. Roessler, a member of the St. Louis Schuetzenverein, designed it in 1913 about the time this kind of shooting was dying out. It is of cast brass with a lathe-turned wood handle. These tools were made with a long removable primer magazine. Primers were advanced by gravity plus the weight of a metal follower. A more detailed description of this tool is presented in the January-February 1981 issue of the *American Single Shot Rifle News.*

The Evans Repeating Rifle Company of Mechanic Falls, Maine produced a very interesting rifle. Their lever action model made in the 1870's, used an archimedean screw in the magazine to feed 34 cartridges of .44 Evans caliber into the action. The new model fired a longer, more powerful cartridge resulting in a somewhat reduced magazine capacity. In (U) is shown an unmarked but unquestionably Evans two-cavity bullet mold/capper. Judging from the cavity, it is for the New Model cartridge. It is made entirely of iron with a blued finish.

U

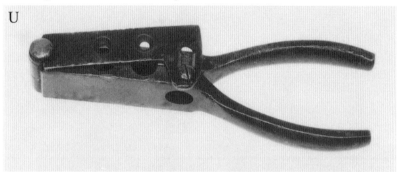

V

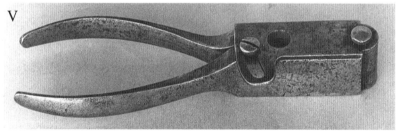

The single cavity mold shown in (V) is unidentified. Like the Evans and some percussion molds, it has distinctly bowed handles. The only markings are the caliber "No .38" and, inside each block and on the sprue plate, "5" suggesting the latter are assembly numbers. The use of "No." to denote caliber was an early practice and its "heel" bullet is also characteristic of an earlier period.

A quite scarce but well marked mold is shown in (W). It is marked "MAN ' F ' D BY" on one handle and " U. S. CAR-TRIDGE CO." on the other. Both specimens examined are in .45-70 caliber; one designed for hollow point bullets. Neither has a caliber marking. With it is shown the loading tool section of the company's broadsheet ad of about 1882. These outfits with several lathe-turned components were produced by many companies. The mold, though included in the price list, does not appear on the sheet.

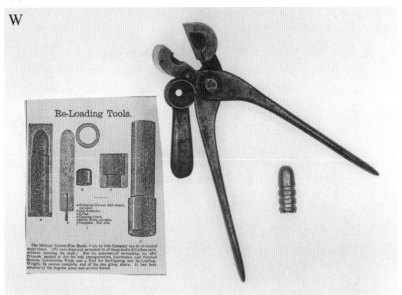

The mold shown in (X) is typical of the C. D. Ladd-type but interestingly is stamped "Remington," "No 5561" and "40 cal." The four digit number suggests manufacture/sale by a company like the Bridgeport Gun Implement Company which used numbers in its catalog descriptions and on some tools. With it is a template for making paper patches also marked "40" and a patch knife. Patches were usually cut diagonally and of a length such that, when wrapped twice around the bullet, the edges would come together but not overlap.

The next three items are from the shop of Walter Cooper who operated the "Montana Armory" in Boseman, Montana from 1870 to 1886. The mold shown in (Y) is of iron and has the shape of an oversized Winchester mold. Another is identical but

X

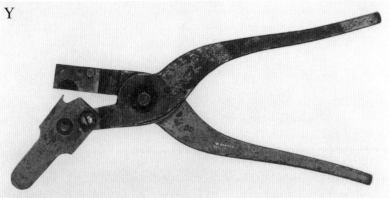

Y

unmarked and may have been made after the business was acquired by the Gottschalk Brothers in 1886.

Another type of Cooper mold, this one for paper patched bullets, is shown in (Z). It is notably similar to some Sharps and very early Winchester molds. The material is brass with a steel cutoff. Stamping on the side tells us that it casts a .40 caliber bullet weighing 195 grains. Protruding from the base is a hollow pointing attachment. This is a very light bullet for .40 caliber but there was a lot of interest among hunters of the period in so-called "express" cartridges using very heavy charges of powder to drive rather light bullets usually of hollow point design. They traded accuracy and sometimes penetration for velocity and im-

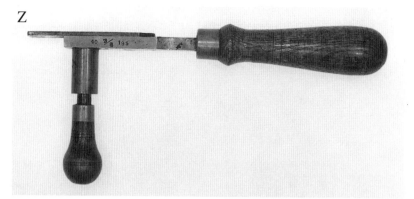

pact. The .45-125 and the .50-95 Winchester are examples of factory express cartridges.

Shown in (AA) is a Cooper case sizer. Constant firing caused cases to swell slightly and, while they were still able to be pushed into the chamber, they worked better if they were not quite so tight. This was especially important with hunters where quick reloading of the rifle, usually a single shot, was important. Also, after sizing, they would be of factory dimensions and could be used in other arms of the same caliber.

AA

The next several items are products of the early twentieth century and are included for their inherent interest and collectibility though they are serviceable as well.

Pictured in (BB) is a loading tool marked "Savage Arms Co., Utica, New York, USA." Its die is stamped with the caliber; in this case ".32-40." Some, probably the earliest ones, have the caliber marked on the body of the tool, a disadvantage because the dies are interchangeable. Savage called it their Model 1904. Inside the box cover was the statement "Adjustable for all lengths of shells and bullets. A powerful and convenient tool." The adjustment referred to the die which is adjustable for both crimp

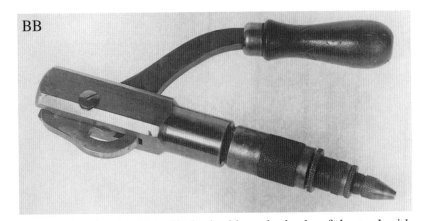

and seating depth. This die locked into the body of the tool with four sturdy lugs like interrupted threads. Calibers offered were .303 Savage, .30-30, .32-40, .25-35, and .38-55. Like the Winchester Model 1894 tool which it resembles, capping was done at the top. Savage alluded to the Winchester tool when they reminded the reloader there are ".... no tedious slow movements to operate." A Savage instruction sheet is shown in (CC). The Savage Arms Company had an agreement with the Ideal Manufacturing Company before the Model 1904 tool came out. Ideal offered what it called "Savage Ideal Reloading Tools" which were regular Ideal tools in .303 Savage and .30-30 calibers, and later in .22 High Power. Savage continued to offer Ideal tools concurrently with the Model 1904 tool. The Savage 1900 catalog even included the Ideal Cylindrical Adjustable Mould for paper patched bullets presumably for use in loading the .303 Paper Patched Schuetzen Target Cartridge illustrated in that catalog.

The United States Government manufactured a great variety of loading implements. They are usually very well made. Two have been selected for inclusion here, For further information, the reader is directed to the extensive research done by James Zupan in *Tools, Targets, and Troopers*. Both these items are from the early 1900's.

In (DD) we see a U. S. government brass gang mold. It casts five .30 caliber round balls designed for very short ranges, often indoors and called "gallery" target shooting, in the .30-40 Krag and in the recently adopted .30-03 Springfield. The bottom

SAVAGE RELOADING TOOLS.

Tool Complete (without mold), cap
extractor and charge cup included, **$3.00**

Price. Die only, $2.00.

"A"—Shell Die.
"B"—Crimper.
"C"—Crimper Ring.
"D"—Bullet Seater.
"E"—Bullet Seater Ring.
"F"—Body.
"G"—Lever.
"H"—Re-capper.

Instructions for Reloading of Cartridges.

First remove exploded primer by placing the cap extractor in the die "A." See that the bullet seater "D" is adjusted at its right length and locked with its ring "E." Insert the shell die "A" into the body "F," turn to the right and the die becomes locked. Take care that the point of the cap extractor is fitted into the primer hole of the empty shell. Then press on the lever sufficiently to remove the primer.

To resize if necessary, wipe shell over with a slightly oiled cloth and place in die "A." Replace the die in tool as above described and operate lever "G." The powerful leverage cams the plug inside the body "F" DIRECTLY on the head of the shell, thus forcing it into the die and resizing the shell so that it will readily chamber in the rifle barrel. This operation is done with ONE MOVEMENT of the lever and the fact that the die "A" containing the shell can be instantly placed in position allows of the most **rapid and satisfying results.** There is no tedious slow screw movements to operate. The backward movement of the lever extracts the shell from the die.

To recap, start the new primer in its pocket, place the shell in position "H" and press home with the lever. Care should be taken that the primer is seated at its fullest depth.

To load a cartridge, charge shell with powder, seat bullet in mouth of shell and place the cartridge in die "A." Adjust crimper "B"—to crimp or not to crimp as desired—and lock same with its ring "C." Adjust bullet seated to the right length locking same with ring "E." After pressing bullet home reverse lever, remove die and the cartridge will drop out. The end of bullet seater "D" is beveled and can be used to open mouths of shells as required. Any variety of bullet may be used and the same seated by proper adjustment.

CAUTION!

Never let die "A" accumulate dirt or rust, keep slightly oiled. Do not experiment with powder charges, especially high pressure smokeless.

Do not let shells corrode, to successfully reload these should be perfectly clean both inside and outside.

When resizing do not attempt to reload with bullet and powder charge, or visa versa.

Miss-fires are apt to occur if the primer is not fully seated.

Do not mutilate the base of a bullet by forcing it into the contracted mouth of a shell.

To properly prepare ammunition and secure accurate results, conditions must be right—therefore go at the matter intelligently.

The completeness of each tool and the rapidity of manipulation are the great advantages of the Savage Reloader.

SPECIAL NOTICE!

This is the only tool that is adjustable **without extra parts** to remove exploded primer, reduce the shell and reload each and every cartridge for which it is made. Each tool complete in itself. Target shooters and hunters will appreciate this reloader as it permits of their experimenting in the different lengths and varieties of bullets.

Can be furnished in the following calibers: .303, 30-30, 25-35, 32-40 and 38-55.

Savage Molds, Charge Cups, Etc.

Price,
10 Cents Each.

Cap Extractor
25 Cents.

Price, $1.10 Each.

Special Cover
for holding Melt-
ing Pot. Will fit
any stove
Price, 50c.

Melting Pot.
Cut ¼ size.
Price, 50c.

is marked "Frankford Arsenal 1904 Cal. .30" with the inspector's initials. This type of mold is also found "cherried" to cast .45 caliber round balls for the .45-70. As with most government arsenal products, it is closely fitted and finely finished. Such items may have been available for National Guard units as well as on

DD

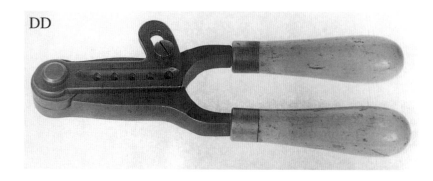

EE

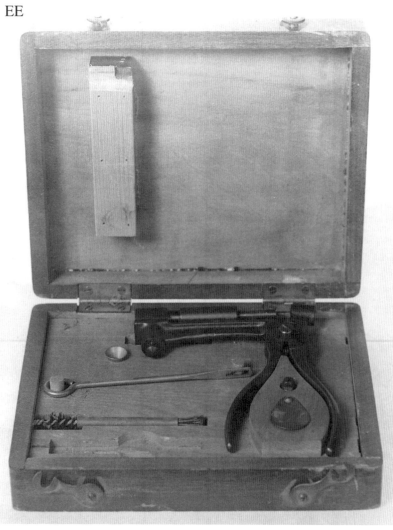

regular Army posts to encourage target practice.

The other arsenal product is a very elaborate outfit whose only purpose was the decapping of fired cases. It is shown in (EE). They appeared about 1907. The main tool is shaped like a pair of pliers but having a spindle on which the fired shell was slipped and the handles closed. Such leverage was desirable with the heavy, crimped-in primers. A small metal funnel was used to guide a cleaning brush into the case. Another brush cleaned the primer pocket. The set is contained in a handsome, fitted, and stained wood case. While brought out for the new .30-06 cartridge, it could also decap the .30-40 Krag, .38 revolver, and, with an adapter, .45 pistol cases.

Now we examine two massive bronze nutcracker-style tools. The one shown in (FF) is made by the Bond Manufacturing Company of Wilmington, Delaware. The caliber, though not marked on either the tool or the dies, is apparently .30-06. A case mouth reamer extends beyond the seating die. The rimless case is held for capping by an ingenious partially segmented ring in the lower handle. There is an adjacent hole for a sizing die, but both it and its plunger are absent suggesting that only jacketed bullets were to be loaded.

Also of bronze is the obviously related (GG). It is marked

FF

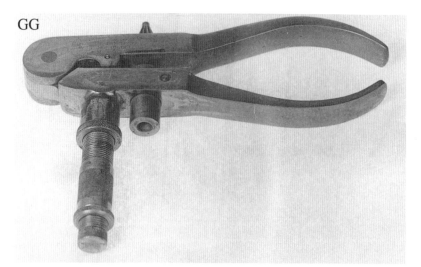

"Modern Bond Co., Wilmington, Del." In light of the improved and simplified design, it is probably the successor to the one just shown. No caliber is marked on either the tool or dies but it reloads .38 special ammunition. Its case mouth reamer is on the top. Because it loads lead bullets, there is a bullet sizer utilizing the capping orifice. The shiny bronze body has a protective coat of clear lacquer applied to it.

HH

Last of the "modern" tools to be considered is shown in (HH). It is the product of the Newton Arms Company and is packaged in a sturdy cardboard tube with metal ends and the directions printed around the outside. Called "the father of high velocity" by one writer, Newton was a better designer than businessman and his company died away in a few years. In addition to his bolt action rifle, he designed a line of ultra powerful cartridges. His tools bear no markings, not even the caliber. These tools are compact, of excellent workmanship, and beautifully blued with a casehardened link.

A bullet mold of the not too distant past is this Yankee. (II) It bears no identification except that some have a six digit number like molds from the Ideal Manufacturing Co. It is of brass with distinctive wood handles. Instead of ferrules the handles are tightly encircled by a fine wire which is twisted and folded down against the underside. There is a lubrication hole at the hinge as found on Pope and some other molds. The Yankee Specialty Company who manufactured these molds was located in Erie, Pennsylvania.

These and other tools and molds of the semi-modern era ought to be the subject of serious research, publication, and collecting as well as occasional use. Most will still do a fine job of reloading if the operator is not rushed.

II

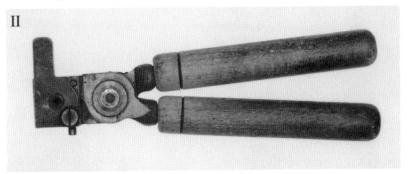

APPENDIX

A Selection of Patent Drawings

W. W. WETMORE.
CARTRIDGE RELOADING IMPLEMENT

No. 376,930.   Patented Jan. 24, 1888.

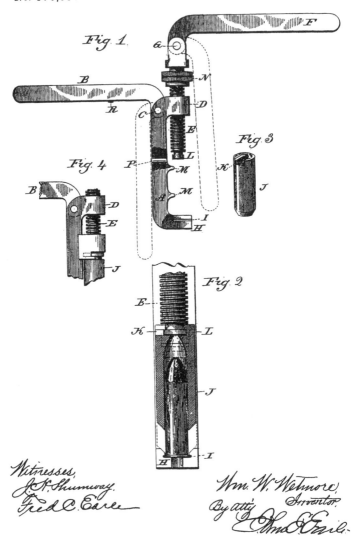

Fig. 1.

Fig. 3.

Fig. 4.

Fig. 2.

Witnesses,
J. K. Shumway.
Fred C. Earle.

Wm. W. Wetmore,
Inventor.
By atty

R. PETERS. Photo-Lithographer, Washington, D. C.

F. J. RABBETH.
POWDER FLASK.

No. 404,932.   Patented June 11, 1889.

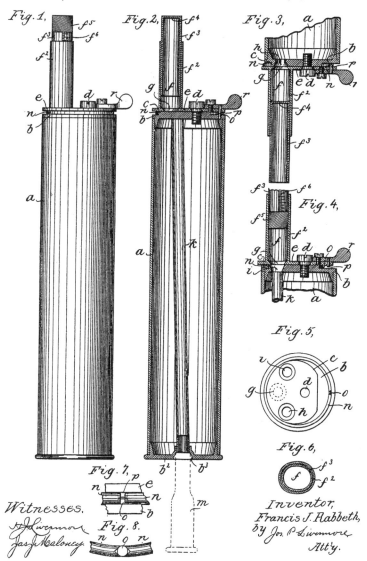

Fig. 1, Fig. 2, Fig. 3, Fig. 4, Fig. 5, Fig. 6, Fig. 7, Fig. 8,

Witnesses.

Inventor,
Francis J. Rabbeth,
by Jos. P. Livermore
Att'y.

G. W. HADLEY.

IMPLEMENT FOR CAPPING AND UNCAPPING CARTRIDGE SHELLS.

No. 310,583. Patented Jan. 13, 1885.

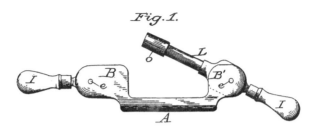

Fig.1.

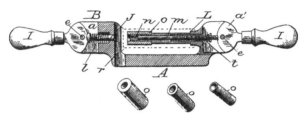

Fig. 2.

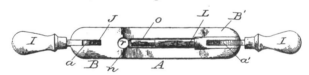

Fig. 3.

Witnesses:

Jas. F. DuHamel.
Walter S. Dodge.

Inventor:

Geo. W. Hadley
by Dodger Son
Attys.

N. PETERS, Photo-Lithographer, Washington, D. C.

148

J. H. BARLOW.
CARTRIDGE IMPLEMENT.

No. 309,681. Patented Dec. 23, 1884.

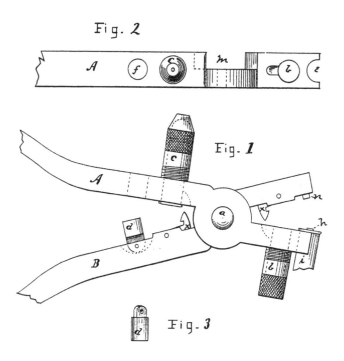

Fig. 2

Fig. 1

Fig. 3

WITNESSES:

George R. Cooley
Robert L. Hazard

INVENTOR
John H. Barlow
BY
L. S. Day
ATTORNEY

J. H. BARLOW.
CARTRIDGE RELOADING TOOL.

No. 267,130.   Patented Nov. 7, 1882.

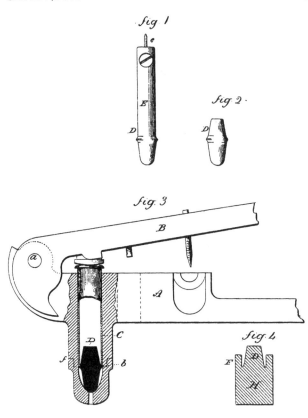

fig. 1

fig 2.

fig. 3

fig. 4

Witnesses,
J. H. Shumway
Jos. C. Earle

John H. Barlow
Inventor
By atty.

J. H. BARLOW.
CARTRIDGE IMPLEMENT.

No. 294,955.   Patented Mar. 11, 1884.

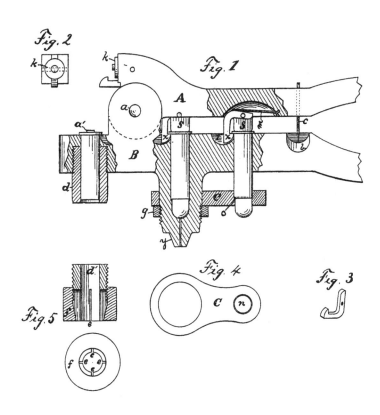

INVENTOR
John H. Barlow
BY L. F. Day
ATTORNEY

(No Model.)

J. M. & M. S. BROWNING.

CARTRIDGE LOADING IMPLEMENT.

No. 247,881. Patented Oct. 4, 1881.

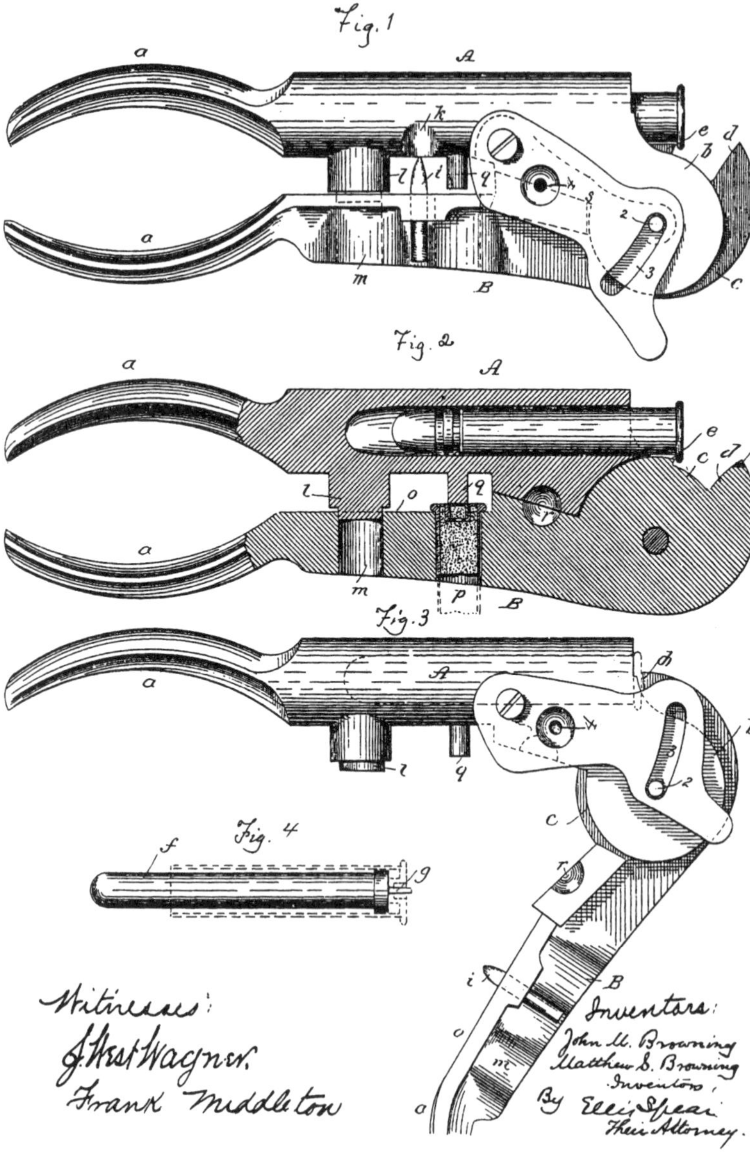
Fig. 1
Fig. 2
Fig. 3
Fig. 4
Witnesses:
J. West Wagner.
Frank Middleton
Inventors:
John M. Browning
Matthew S. Browning
Inventors,
By Ellis Spear
Their Attorney.

N. PETERS, Photo-Lithographer, Washington, D.C.

V. A. KING.
Cartridge Implement.

No. 232,189.   **Patented Sept. 14, 1880.**

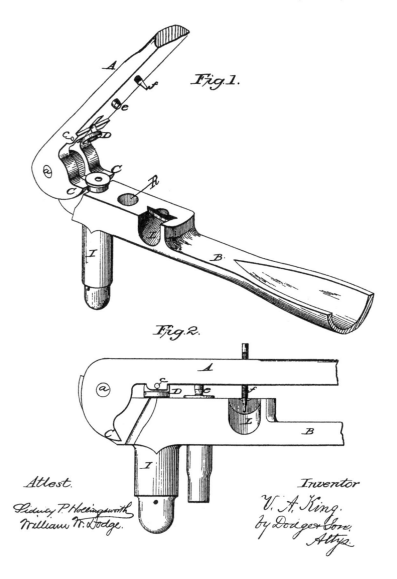

Fig.1.

Fig.2.

Atlest.

Sidney P. Hollingsworth.
William W. Dodge.

Inventor

V. A. King.
by Dodge Son.
Attys.

H. PETERS, PHOTO-LITHOGRAPHER, WASHINGTON, D. C.

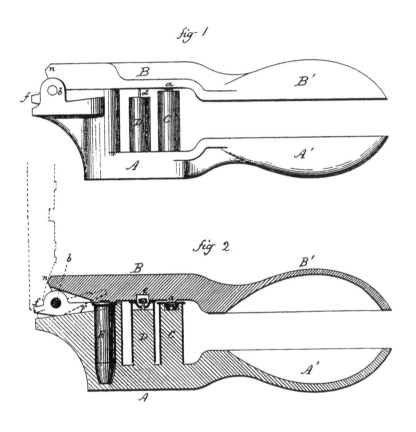

fig. 1

fig. 2

Wm. W. Winchester
Inventor
By Attys.
John S. Earle

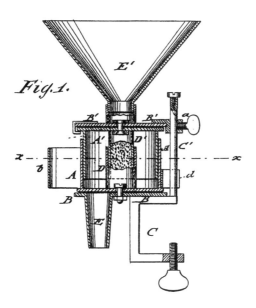

Fig. 1.

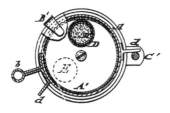

Fig. 2.

C. H. GRIFFITH.
CARTRIDGE RELOADING IMPLEMENT.

No. 448,228.   Patented Mar. 17, 1891.

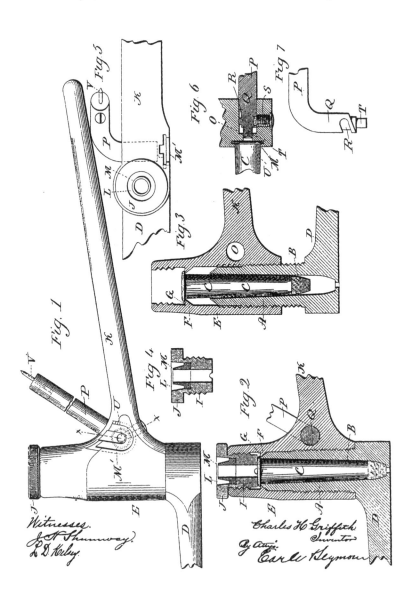

Witnesses.
J. H. Shumway
L. D. Kelsey

Charles H. Griffith
Inventor
By atty.
Earle Seymour

(No Model.)

J. H. BARLOW.
BULLET MOLD.

No. 446,178. Patented Feb. 10, 1891.

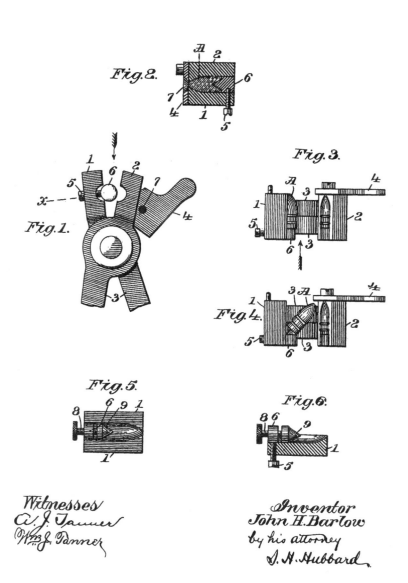

Fig.2.

Fig.1.

Fig.3.

Fig.4.

Fig.5.

Fig.6.

Witnesses
C. J. Tanner
W. J. Tanner

Inventor
John H. Barlow
by his attorney
S. H. Hubbard

J. H. BARLOW.
BULLET MOLD.

No. 489,580.

Patented Jan. 10, 1893.

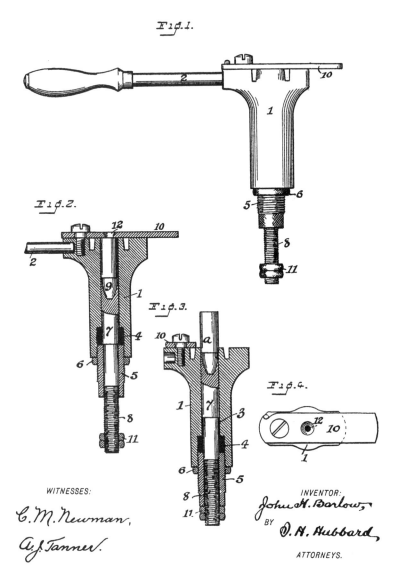

Fig.1.

Fig.2.

Fig.3.

Fig.4.

WITNESSES:

C. M. Newman,

A. J. Tanner.

INVENTOR:

John H. Barlow,

BY D. H. Hubbard

ATTORNEYS.

W. MASON.
CARTRIDGE RELOADING IMPLEMENT.

No. 514,722.

Patented Feb. 13, 1894.

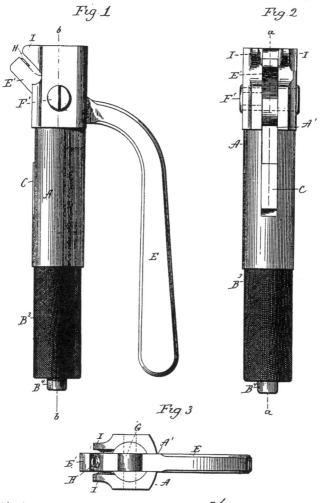

Fig 1

Fig 2

Fig. 3

(No Model.)

J. H. BARLOW.
DECAPPING AND RECAPPING TOOL.

No. 486,659.   Patented Nov. 22, 1892.

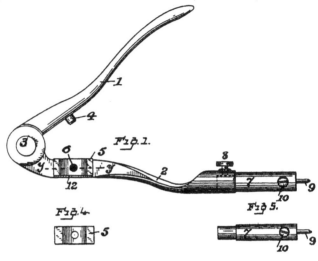

Fig. 1.

Fig. 5.

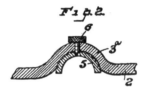

Fig. 4.

5

Fig. 2.

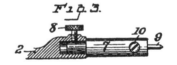

Fig. 3.

Witnesses.
A. J. Tanner.
M. E. Hinchcliffe.

Inventor,
John H. Barlow
By his attorney
O. N. Hubbard

J. H. BARLOW.
BULLET SIZER.

No. 464,311.   **Patented Dec. 1, 1891.**

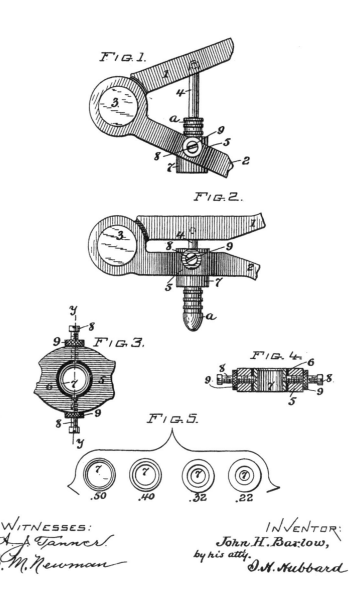

Fig.1.

Fig.2.

Witnesses:

Donn P. Twitchell.
S. M. Madden.

Inventor:

Geo. W. Hadley
By his atty.
Dodgersen

H. A KINGSLAND.
Implement for Capping and Uncapping Cartridges.

No. 202,831.   Patented April 23, 1878.

Fig.1.   Fig.2.

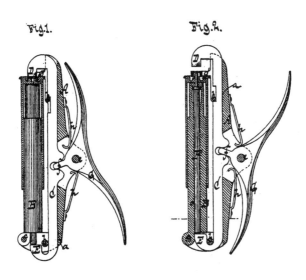

Fig.3.

Witnesses.
Otto Hepland.
Hugo Brueggemann

Inventor.
Hugh A. Kingsland
by Van Santvoord & Hauff
his attorneys

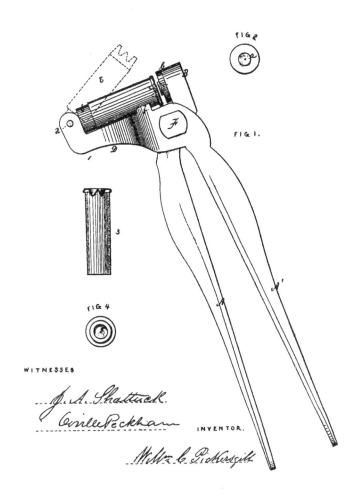

FIG 2

FIG 1.

FIG 4

WITNESSES

J. A. Shattuck.

Orille Peckham

INVENTOR.

Will. C. Pickersgill

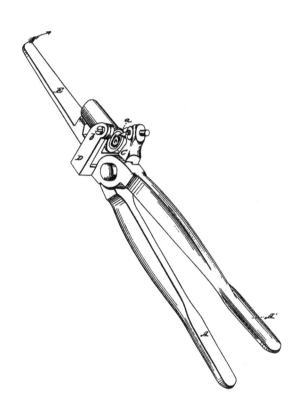

Witnesses
W. A. Crandall.
William B. Dart.

Inventor
Willm C Pickersgill

W. C. PICKERSGILL.

Apparatus for Setting Bullets in Cartridges.

No. 97,806.

Patented Dec. 14, 1869.

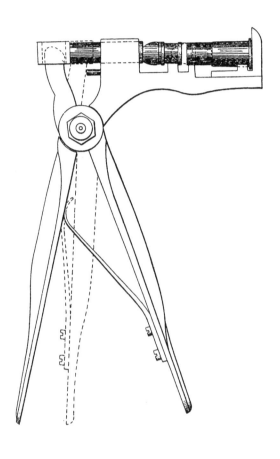

WITNESSES

J. A. Shattuck

Orville Beckham

INVENTOR

Willm C Pickersgill

H. PETERS, Photo-Lithographer, Washington, D. C.

H. A. LYON.
CARTRIDGE IMPLEMENT.

No. 378,400.　　　　　　　Patented Feb. 21, 1888.

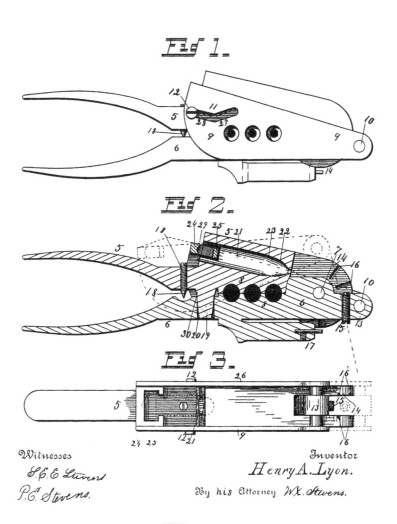

Witnesses

S. C. E. Stevens

P. C. Stevens.

Inventor

Henry A. Lyon.

By his Attorney W. X. Stevens.